CREATIVE AND CONNECTED

By Leigh Shannon
Early Childhood Consultant
Joni Samples, EdD
©2019

DEDICATION

We dedicated this book to Marian Gage. Her work as a drug prevention specialist and positive youth developer, during the formative years of Creative and Connected© was a source of knowledge, encouragement and hope. And now, with her assistance as editor for this revision, Marian-five years into her retirement-continues to volunteer her time and expertise for suffering children.

FORWARD

Introduction to the Developers

Leigh: I am excited to share Creative and Connected with you, and for you to get to know me. Studying classical ballet-and performing-from age nine to adulthood, I decided then to teach ballet. Later, I got deeply involved in the field of Child Development and exploring related fields of psychology and psychiatry. I have taught at California State University, Chico, University of California, Davis, and Brigham Young University. The goal of applying that knowledge to the field of dance was my intent.

After marriage and the birth of my children, I had the rare experience of learning from Professor of Child Development, Roma Winn, giving me hand on training with each of my five children.

Another milestone was discovering Dr. Asahel Woodruff.s work on concepts, in my university library. Doing an in-depth study of his work, including face-to-face interviews with Dr. Woodruff in his lab at the University of Utah, I learned how to apply concepts to teaching movement to preschoolers. These children easily learned concepts such as tempo, emotional feeling, rhythm, etc., through their natural language of movement.

Additionally, I began researching creativity; what it is, examples in nature, in life. Could creativity be taught to preschool children? After much research seeking answers to these questions, the creative process became clear and I applied it to my work. Three of the five steps will be used in this curriculum. They are: Aware, Explore, Improvise.

The first step is to help children become Aware of themselves and others by Exploring and then Improvising through body movements. As children become aware they can move a specific part of the body, they can then begin to explore patterns of their own improvised movement.

Having worked with young children ages 3-5 for many years, including children at-risk, I am convinced of the importance of preschool facilitators and teachers in the support of positive development of the whole child. To address the wholeness, I arrived at four domains: feeling, cognition, psycho-motor and mindfullness. Providing activities in these domains within both an environment of structured and free play supports the preschoolers sense of safety enabling them to feel more comfortable to express themselves while interacting with others. I am so grateful to present to you Creative and Connected, a curriculum that will provide you some wonderful positive development tools that now includes a link to current brain research. Both Joni and I are so appreciative of you, Facilitators and teachers of preschool children, for your willingness to join us in this most important task of positively developing our future generations.

Joni: I knew I wanted to be a teacher when I was seven years old. I never wavered. It's what I wanted to do and what I've always done starting as a teacher's aide while I was in college and finishing my public service career as a superintendent. Along the way, I taught both regular education students as well as students with special needs. I currently teach family engagement, brain work and other things that I'm interested in. I'd rather teach than just about anything.

I started studying the brain and brain development when I was working on my Doctorate at Northern Arizona University. I had been teaching special needs children, particularly the learning disabled, and kept wondering what was different from one child's brain to another. When I first started, I could have learned everything available on brain education by taking one college class. Now, there are discoveries coming out weekly and I'm enjoying all of the new work in the field.

For this project, I was excited for the new opportunities to incorporate the focus of brain development and learning with Leigh's work because it fits so well. This is especially true working with children at-risk for problems in their lives related to the current crises for adult opioid addiction and violence. I feel so encouraged that Creative and Connected provides strategies to work with these at-risk children along with their peers. Current brain research shows how the crises of addiction can negatively impact children, including the brain being underdeveloped. That underdevelopment is a crisis in itself. We want to help remedy these influences.

Please use Creative and Connected with our best intentions and wishes for yours and our precious children's lives. The following pages provide background information regarding the components and philosophies of the Creative and Connected program. It is important to study this information as it provides additional Facilitator insight and methods needed to successfully execute this curriculum.

The developers feel strongly that it is imperative for Facilitators to follow the curriculum lessons faithfully as written. Please do not use substitutions, improvisation, or adaptations so that you may achieve similar results as the developer. For example: using live flowers vs silk flowers may seem insignificant, but for children to be able to explore and express creativity and beauty in the most real way, these instructions are extremely critical.

Leigh and Joni are so thankful for you who are willing to take on the huge task of learning and applying a new program to protect our nation's most valuable resource…its children. In building young children's feelings of positive self-confidence, connectedness and safety—sometimes so absent from their lives—we promise you joy and contentment as you do this work.

We are extremely grateful to those who have supported and taught us, often in the most difficult of circumstance, to understand the needs of young children. Our hearts especially go out to those children affected by opioid, other drugs, alcohol, and violence crises. We are humbled, and so appreciative, to share this important work of shaping young children with you.

This book is written in secular format. This curriculum addresses the Connection in a way that you may use for the children you serve. Please enjoy.

Table of Contents

I. Components of CREATIVE AND CONNECTED

II. Developers' Experience, Background and Perspective

III. Creative and Connected Key Components

IV. Lessons One-Fourteen

V. Glossary of Brain Terms

VI. Bibliography

IMPORTANT NOTE: Lessons 7, 11, and 12 contain the sensitive subjects of sexual abuse, violence, and addiction. Before these lessons are presented parent/ guardian permission will be needed to discuss such subjects with their children.

CREATIVE AND CONNECTED©
By Leigh Shannon and Dr. Joni Samples

The Core Goal of Creative and Connected is to address all children, especially children at-risk and in emotional pain, by creating an atmosphere of safety that will support young children's positive development. This will be accomplished by providing activities that help the child explore self-identify through body movement with classical music, learn about feelings and how to deal with them, and how to positively interact with others. We achieve this goal through structured safe activities that address the following four domains:

- **Feeling** — Learning how to identify emotions and positively navigate them

- **Cognition** — Learning to think about their surroundings, others, and how to think first in resolving conflict

- **Psycho-Motor** — Learning how the body moves and how that movement can be used for self-expression

- **Mindfulness** — Learning a sense of self and the beauty within, sense of others, sense of beauty in nature, classical music, and sense of love and peace.

Each Creative and Connected activity reflects the creative process for exploring the four domains through the following progressive steps:

1. First: Becoming aware through the exploration of body movements, feelings, interactions with the Facilitators/teachers and other children

2. Second: Becoming comfortable in a safe environment to explore individual and interactive expressions of body movements and feelings.

3. Third: Becoming proficient in the self-expression of body movements and feelings and an exploration of the world around them.

FOCUS

This curriculum was developed to serve all three; four- and five-year-old children of diverse backgrounds.

Creative and Connected© is a positive intervention for children who are at risk.

DEVELOPERS' EXPERIENCE, BACKGROUND AND PERSPECTIVE

Leigh: Thirty years ago, when I began writing curriculum for young children, I organized my work around three domains: cognition (thinking), affect (feeling), and psychomotor (body movement). Years later, when our culture began changing, I became aware of the need for curricula that would have life-changing impact. Working with my mentors, Dr. Asahel Woodruff, Prof. Roma Winn and Dr. Ron Lowe, I began constantly associating the three domains in my curricula, discovering the positive impact on children's self-confidence in a way I had not thought possible. Pre-school children could readily perceive and apply abstract concepts such as emotional feelings, direction, level, rhythm and concentrate for long stretches of time. They would feel exhilarated with their own creativity, while working interdependently with their peers' creativity. Working with prevention consultant Marian Gage, I became aware of some children who seemed to have difficulties in this positive development. These children often came from difficult situations at home. They were considered at-risk children. As a result I developed a Fourth Domain called mindfullness—sense of self and others and the beauty within, sense of beauty in nature and in classical music, a sense of inner peace, and love.

Now having worked with children ages 3 through 5 for many years, and especially children at-risk, it is my conviction that how activities that address the four domains are scheduled, is also very important. Resiliency research shows that some children seem to be able to be resilient even in the midst of major stressors, but many can't. Alternating free play (child's choice) and structured activity (Facilitator/teacher choice) is not only developmentally correct, but contributes to the child's feeling of security. As the child moves toward the development of wholeness, there is less resistance and eventually, an enthusiasm for the Facilitator/teacher's activity. Having structure makes a child feel more comfortable and safe to express his/her creativity.

This curriculum helps develop wholeness for children through activities that build positive self-confidence and capacity in their individual self-awareness and positive interaction with others. Building positive self-identity is especially important for those at-risk children affected by opioid use, other addictions, and difficult situations. It allows children to discover their own and other's uniqueness and enhances the experience of joy. When all four domains are constantly associated in a developmentally appropriate curriculum, new skills are developed that expands new brain neuron networks, generating capacities that can support positive identity, brain functioning, and self-confidence.

The Facilitators of this curriculum will be enriched and surprised as they witness the wonder of the child's unfolding development of positive self-identity and wholeness. The Facilitators will be privy, day by day, to the child's unique creativity, see the self-confidence emerge, and the fragmented little person gradually becoming positively connected to him/herself and others, resulting in wholeness.

CREATIVE AND CONNECTED AND OUR DEVELOPING BRAINS

Joni: This curriculum was created and tried-successfully by the way-30 years ago, but I was drawn to and became excited about Creative and Connected© in regard to the curriculum's relevance to more recent research on the brain that reflects scientific findings on why this type of program has been so successful.

Most recently I have become concerned about the huge upsurge of adult opiate use and the possible effect on child development. Drug abuse came to national attention with Prohibition, focusing on the use of alcohol. Alcohol abuse continued as a focus due to deaths related to drinking-and-driving accidents. It wasn't until the 1970's substance abuse epidemic that started the war on drugs (i.e., marijuana, uppers, downers, pain killers, cigarettes, workaholism, domestic violence, sexual proclivities or any number of other issues). However, the recent problems of over use of opiates, often prescribed drugs, is having a major impact. This certainly effects the adult population, but what of the children? What happens to a child who is living in a family, no matter what the family structure, where one of these substances is being abused?

The research of drug addiction over the past 40 years has revealed how addiction has major detrimental impacts on brain development, functioning, and brain chemistry. Drug abusers may have damaged their brain chemistry to such an extent that they may need prescribed drugs, just to feel normal, for the rest of their lives. They lose their natural brain capacity to feel pleasure and to deal with pain. They also stunt their brain capacity for developing normal emotional and social skills. Think of the difficulties these folks have in trying to parent. Additional research on the effects of children witnessing violence has shown how this negative influence can hamper the normal development of a child's brain that can impair decision-making and emotional development.

I began to focus on the big question. How does living with a parent having some issues, whatever they might be, affect a child's brain development? I was so pleased to be introduced to Leigh and this curriculum that attempts to address this emotion. I am excited to include in this curriculum the brain research and information I have gained as an educator. As we learn more about the brain, we find how little we are educated about it. Creative and Connected© includes different types of information regarding a child's development in support of brain education. We will talk about brain parts, how they work and what affects the development both positively and negatively. We have learned that the brain is affected by repetition. Repeated events bring about changes in the brain development related to whatever those events are. Repeated abuse brings about fear. Repeated love and security bring about confidence and ability to make decisions. Repeated connection to mindfullness transform an adults life as well as a child's. I have personal experience to assure you of that.

Your role as Facilitator/teacher is so important in the positive development of a child's brain that can have positive, impact even for the at-risk child. As you implement this curriculum, you will find activities and suggestions that can be used in order to further brain development in a positive way. Parents and teachers have a huge impact on both the "hardware and software" of the brain. As an educator, my vision is to develop the best operating systems that will provide outstanding programs for the optimal development of every child's brain so that he/she may have the best joy-filled, productive life.

Brain Connections: Look for the Brain Connection box. They're located in the Purposes section before each lesson. The purpose of the brain connection is to answer the consistent question—how does what the lesson gives you to do, affect brain development in a child? This connection is truly vital in helping a child become the authentic whole person he/she can be. Please know why, from a brain standpoint, you are doing what you do.

For Example:

Brain Connections: And here's an extra brain box to show you how this works. Did you know adult brains are different than children's brain? A young child has many more neural development possibilities than adults. There are as many as 100 billion neurons in a baby's brain. Neurons are "pruned" or trimmed away if they aren't used. As adults there are many neural pathways that we may have never used and they have disappeared. For example, we may not have learned Swahili, or how to ice skate, or how to play the piano. If we don't use them, we lose them. Can you learn things as you get older? Absolutely. I have a good friend learning a fourth language. She learned three as a child and that was so easy. This one is harder. Yes, those neurons were pruned years ago, but creating new neurons is absolutely possible and why we can learn new things, no matter what they are.

And now for the curriculum itself

Welcome to Creative and Connected

MOVEMENT, THE LANGUAGE OF CHILDREN

Talking, walking, running, standing, touching, singing, climbing, playing-the pre-school child is constantly moving. During sleep, the child may turn pull up his legs, fling out an arm, or move his head. In that enviable state of deep sleep when completely relaxed and still, vital movements inside his body keep his heart beating, blood circulating, digestion flowing, lungs breathing. Even before birth, the fetus is moving and those vital movements develop the brain, the nerves, and the muscles. After birth, the young baby expresses him/herself through movement, and these movements signal the mother about the young baby's needs and feelings. Long before speech begins, the young child communicates through the movement medium. Movement (the psycho-motor domain) is the language of children. For the child, movement is not only the most familiar, but the safest choice for a medium of expression. It is a guiltless way to communicate what's going on inside.

When movement is used to teach concepts, young children will learn abstract concepts efficiently, such as emotional feelings, and apply these concepts as part of their lives. Movement is the inherent channel into the beauty and creativity that is lodged within all children. Surprising progress in positive self-identity occurs as the child, through movement, taps into and expresses his inner beauty and creativity.

Movement is an international language, as all children move regardless of their culture and ethnicity. Movement, therefore, can be used as a key communication tool with diverse groups of children. Using the movement/kinesthetic modality for self-expression is unique to CREATIVE AND CONNECTED©.

SINGING

Singing children's songs of joy is fun for children. Singing encourages. Singing uplifts. Singing brings hope. Songs can be used to help children connect to their self-confidence, as well as to stimulate positive brain activity and development. This is the reason why each Creative and Connected lesson begins and ends with a song, a vital activity for this curriculum.

Facilitator/teachers of this curriculum are strongly encouraged to sing these two songs during other parts of the pre-school day: for example, circle time, transitions, outside, during music time, etc.

RECORDING BEHAVIOR

We recommend that the Facilitator/teacher focus on one behavior at a time for each child they work with, if possible. Of course, it makes sense to begin working first on extinguishing behaviors that hurt other children. This will not be accomplished quickly. It will take time, since this behavior may be an at-risk child's cry for help to deal with their emotional pain. Little by little progress will occur, but behavior must be recorded to see small gains, to measure progress. Recording children's behaviors, will also allow the Facilitator/teacher to see the progress toward wholeness in a child.

A small notebook and pencil can be tucked into a pocket and carried around with the Facilitator/teacher for that purpose. When a child exhibits the behavior the teacher is working to extinguish, the teacher notes the time and a word or two of description. For example, the child's name is at the top of the page, then "10:03 pushed Jarrell off slide; unprovoked." The total time for recording – four seconds. At-risk children progress a little at a time. At the end of the child's day at pre-school, the teacher tallies the number of times the behavior occurred. The teacher compares it with the child's score the last few days. This factual information then provides insight into the child's progress in that particular behavior. This factual information then gives the teacher the picture. Sometimes with at-risk children it is helpful to start with a behavior that is not the most disruptive-i.e., start small and build on that success. The exception is acting out behavior that is hurting other children, as that will affect the sense of safety in the classroom.

INTERVENTION

We have mentioned compelling reasons why an intervention program is necessary for all pre-school children. Negative influences such as alcohol/drug abuse, violence in the home or neighborhood, or lack of quality family time are putting our children more at risk. In 1992, when this program was originally developed and tested, national statistics revealed that one out of every four homes in America had a substance-abuse problem. In 2014, a national drug abuse survey revealed that 27 million people aged 12 or older used an illicit drug in the past 30 days, which corresponds to about 1 in 10 Americans (10.2 percent). 4.3 million people aged 12 or older reported current nonmedical use of prescription pain relievers. According to the U.S. Census, the number of children being raised by their grandparents skyrocketed from 2.4 million in 2000 to 4.9 million in 2010. Two of the primary causes of this are addiction and mental disorder. Among all of the family members who are impacted by an addict's disease, perhaps no one suffers as much as children. The effects of living with an addicted parent can be felt long after childhood, and well into adulthood. Parental alcoholism and drug addiction can create poor self-image, loneliness, guilt, anxiety, feelings of helplessness, fear of abandonment and chronic depression in children. Maternal substance abuse during pregnancy can also lead to a host of behavioral and developmental disorders in children.

Even in homes free from substance abuse, children may be at risk for substance abuse and delinquency. According to recent studies, our children watch excessive amounts of TV, suggesting that television has become a substitute for human intimacy. With Ipads, computers, phones, and gaming devices now available, potential negative influences from these sources may increase. Low parental involvement and expectations is another risk factor.

In Creative and Connected© there are two intervention strategies included in every lesson. They are: building self-confidence, and exploring and mastering connectedness. Some at-risk children with low self-confidence may be so disconnected that any crisis might cause further alienation and trigger severe trauma. These children's sense of self has been so violated, it is very difficult for them to engage positively in activities or with others. They also have difficulty dealing with emotional pain that results in attention-getting behavior, such as withdrawing, or acting out that demands a lot of the Facilitator/teacher's time to positively engage this child.

Something to consider:

Jerry, who'd just turned five years old, and the youngest of my five children, and Josh, an only child, had just completed two years of preschool.

Josh was the biggest child in the preschool class, and struggled to learn to use words instead of hurting children. With two years of pre-school experience, he had come a long way. Though playing with children occasionally took precedence over the niceties of following rules (such as urinating outside so his playing was not interrupted).

During the summer, Josh would ask his mother to take him to Jerry's house to play. When our doorbell rang I would say, "Jerry, look who came to play with you!" Josh and Jerry happily would greet each other. The next thing I would say was, "Josh, here are the rules: No hitting—use your words. If you decide to hit Jerry, I will call your Mom, and she will come back immediately and take you home. Urinate in the toilet and not outside. Josh, do you understand the rules?" He would answer "yes." (He always followed the rules when he came to our house).

One day when Josh asked again to go to Jerry's house to play, his mother said, "Josh, why don't we have Jerry come here to play?" Josh was adamant—he wanted to go to Jerry's house. His mother asked "Why?" His answer was, "Because Mrs. Shannon is so mean!" The limits and follow-through at my house made Josh feel secure.

IDENTIFYING CHILDREN'S NEEDS

Pre-school children at-risk for delinquency and substance abuse, due to risk previously described, exhibit two extreme behaviors–withdrawal and explosive acting out. There is a continuum of levels between the extremes of these behaviors a child may express. For example, these children may seldom stay on task (poor attention spans), may continually test limits, may have difficulty with spontaneity, may seldom talk or get involved, may have difficulty bonding with other children or the teacher, may hurt others without provocation, and may have difficulty following rules.

These children have holes in their souls as described by John Bradshaw, dysfunctional family system therapist. The holes are caused from the emotional pain related to their unmet needs.

INTERVENTIONS FOR CHILDREN WHO ARE ACTING OUT

Remember, acting-out behaviors can be seen as a cry for help from the emotional pain of an at-risk child. At one end of the acting-out behavior continuum is the child who hits, kicks, bites, pinches (etc.) other children. These behaviors do not serve positive self-development, and need to be intervened upon by, being taught to use words instead. Although a difficult principle that takes time to learn, it is vital in creating more positive connections and relationships.

When a child hurts another child, it becomes necessary for the Facilitator to restrain him/her. There are two ways to do this. One option is to put the child on time-out in a chair, beside the Facilitator. By putting her/his hand on the child's shoulder gently, but firmly, this helps the child to stay in the chair. Sometimes the child will cry or scream, flailing about, to get off the chair. When the child becomes calm and relaxed—ready to listen—the Facilitator may say, "Billy, why are you on time-out?" Billy's response might be, "I don't know."

The Facilitator may ask, "Why was Paul crying? What did you to do Paul?" Then the Facilitator says, "You kicked (hit, bit, etc.) Paul." Then, using eye contact with Billy, with her/his hand still on Billy's shoulder, the Facilitator says, "You may not hurt children. Kicking hurts. You use your words. You can say, "Paul, move over." Then the Facilitator has Billy practice these words two times. The Facilitator calls Paul to come over to her/him and says, "What do you say to Paul about hurting him?" The Facilitator coaches Billy to say to Paul, "I'm sorry I hurt you." The Facilitator will then acknowledge Billy saying, "You did it, Billy-you used your words!" (P.S. Facilitator, make sure you comfort Paul when he gets hurt.)

The second option to restrain a child: The Facilitator can restrain a child (who has hurt another child) by holding his/her hand gently, but firmly, keeping the child right beside her/him. The Facilitator continues doing her/his tasks while holding the child's hand, until the child stops crying and becomes calm. The Facilitator then goes through the dialogue in the example above.

Should the Facilitator get angry at a child when he/she hurts another child, look at the cause of your anger. It may be from the current situation, but it may also be from something in your own past. If you do get angry, the child will sense it. Anger reactions are what the child is used to, so change this destructive behavior loop. It is important not to get angry.

All teachers of young children will have opportunities to work through anger reactions as this is challenging work. One strategy is to ask yourself, "Why did I get angry?" Then list the reasons. You may have to do this several times. This exercise will help you to become aware of your emotional triggers that we all have. Many of them were developed when we were children. Recognizing, knowing, and admitting those triggers, before a child sets them off, can help deter anger reactivity.

Another powerful tool follows. After becoming calm, the Facilitator/teacher acknowledges to a child or class that you lost your cool, and ask the child or class to forgive you. This can be a great teaching moment modeling how to be aware of the hurtful impact of expressing angry feelings and how using words that say "I am sorry," can help develop trust, safety and wholeness.

AFFECTION AND LIMITS WITH CONSEQUENCES

Many teachers and parents struggle with giving a child limits because they don't want to be seen in the role of "meanie" or "heavy." They feel that to give limits one must be negative or angry. Sometimes parents and teachers feel children will not love them if they give firm limits. Actually, love has two dimensions: Affection and limits.

It is important– that limits be consistent—and those limits have appropriate consequences. Sometimes adults can give consequences that are either too light or too harsh for the infraction, or not age-appropriate. If a child receives only affection from a teacher or parent, the child will not feel loved; he/she doesn't feel the parents love him/her because he/she can do whatever he/she wants. It's as if the parent doesn't really care. If the child receives only limits without affection from a teacher or parent, the child will not feel loved…. This is a lesson for the ages…. It's as if the child feels he/she can't do anything right and will never be what the parent wants. A teacher (or parent) must give both affection and consistent limits with appropriate consequences, for a child to feel sure she/he is loved. Affection refers to expressing warmth, devotion, tenderness, interest, follow-through, caring, compassion, and support.

Example I
Teacher says to a child, "Come and tell me how you feel about that. I really want to know."

Example II
Andrew is loudly crying because he has to wait for his turn on the trike. The teacher says, "You're feeling disappointed that it isn't your turn, aren't you? It's hard to wait for your turn, isn't it?"

Another part of expressing love is giving limits with appropriate consequences. Limits refer to setting boundaries so that a child learns what is expected and what is appropriate. Boundaries help keep a child physically safe and emotionally secure.

Example I
Several four-year olds and the Facilitator were doing a Creative and Connected© activity. The children were engaged. At one point, Haseem moved away from the group and began examining a block. The Facilitator immediately returned Haseem to the group, saying, "This is what we are doing now, Haseem." He became involved in the group again. In a few minutes Haseem went over and began looking at a book. The Facilitator took Haseem by the hand and brought

him back to the group, saying to him, "This is what we are doing now. Sit here beside me, please."

Example II

Andrew, an at-risk four-year old, hurt other children routinely without provocation. It was an expression of his emotional pain. The intervention is learning to use words to express pain. When Andrew hurt a child, the teacher would make hand-eye contact and say, "People are not for hurting, Andrew. You can hit a stuffed animal or the punching bag, but not people. You can say, "I'm mad!" But hurting people is not allowed. Sit here until you decide to stop hurting people." (Lessons that address coping skills for the expressing of anger are included in this curriculum.) When Andrew's attitude changed, evidenced by sitting quietly and listening to the teacher, he was allowed to return to the group, after apologizing to the child he hurt.

Example III

One morning Andrew repeatedly hurt children. The teacher said to him, "Andrew, you are all through playing with the children today. You will stay right beside me until your mommy comes. You may try playing again with the children tomorrow." When Andrew and his mom were leaving, the Facilitator said, "Andrew, you are a smart boy! You will learn to use your words when you feel bad inside." Incidentally, Andrew often would go to the teacher and say, "Teacher, I love you."

Limits with appropriate consequences are as much an expression of love as affection. It takes both for a child to feel loved.

At-risk children test and test limits. This testing is emotionally and physically exhausting for teachers and parents, but it serves a purpose. These children test the limits because they can't trust their environment or the adults taking care of them. They don't believe anyone would care enough to follow through with them. By testing, they learn that a teacher or parent will be there for them. Testing is a way they learn if they are valued, if they are of worth. When the testing eases, you will know they are on their journey toward wholeness and your intervention is a success.

Affection, including consistent limits with appropriate consequences, conveys a powerful message of love. At-risk children, especially, are so in need of both dimensions of love.

ENCOURAGEMENT

Driekurs, a psychiatrist doing studies on children's behavior, tells us that encouragement to a child is like water to a plant. It is life-giving. The principle of encouragement is used in all three sections of this curriculum.

Since at-risk children test repeatedly, encouragement is used to give them hope that they can change their behavior.

Example I

A teacher removes Lisa from the group because she has once again hit and kicked a child near her. The teacher said, "Lisa, when you choose to hurt people, you are choosing to sit over here. You can hurt the stuffed toys, and the bop bag, but not people. You are such a smart girl; you will learn not to hurt people." The teacher is prepared to see that Lisa sits on the chair until the teacher sees a change in her attitude: The child relaxes and listens to the teacher. The encouragement is, "You will learn." Also, encouraging is the teacher's recognition of one of Lisa's strengths, "You are a smart girl," especially when the teacher is enforcing a limit.

Example II

Althea threw sand on the children in the sandbox. As the teacher removed Althea from the sandbox, she said, "Throwing sand can hurt children. You are all through in the sandbox for today. You may try the sandbox again tomorrow."

In both examples, the message is conveyed, "You can do it. I'll give you another chance to work on it. I have confidence in you." Notice: <u>the encouragement does not alter consequences.</u>

When these children begin responding, as they will, due to the interventions, activities and positive actions of the Facilitator/teacher, the teacher will be quick to say, "Lisa, you did it! You did it! You didn't hit! You didn't kick! You yelled, 'I'm mad!' You are learning!!"

SPEAK A LANGUAGE OF FEELINGS

In most families of at-risk children three dysfunctional rules exist: don't talk about feelings, don't talk about important real issues, and don't trust. These children are disconnected from their own and others feelings, from reality, and from trusting themselves and others. These children can be so affected they may view themselves as not existing, or as objects.

Reconnecting these children to their feelings and to trust is vital, for the child to achieve wholeness. Facilitators/teachers can help by speaking a language of feeling and model expressing feelings.

For example: Ask the children, "How did you feel about circle time today?"

"Now that you can put on your coat all by yourself, how does that make you feel?"

"Lemah, did you like it when Mary hit you?" Child responds, "Tell Mary how it made you feel."

"Andrew, was it easy to wait for your turn?"

"Do you like this color, children?"

"Children, how did you feel about art today?"

"Jarrell, did you like singing that song?"

"Haseem, how did you feel when Andrew called you a baby?" Child responds. Facilitator/teacher says, "Go and tell Andrew how you feel when he calls you a baby."

"Did you like this story, Haseem?"

How did you feel about using the scissors today, Jarrell?"

To Andrew, who is shouting, "You're mean" at the teacher: "Andrew, are you feeling mad at me because I stopped you playing with the Legos when you were having fun?" Andrew responds. The teacher says, "It's disappointing to have to stop when you are having fun, isn't it? But it's time to go home."

ENDORSEMENT (Positive Reinforcement)

The purpose of endorsing-the term we use for positive reinforcement-is to recognize effort in a self-complimentary building way. To do this, the endorser describes what is seen, and includes the time when possible.

So often we compliment or endorse people in a way that calls into question the individual's acceptance. For example, "You always say the right thing." No one ALWAYS says the right thing. The statement does imply lack of acceptance when the individual does not say the right thing.

This kind of endorsing or complimenting is burdensome and implies an unacceptance of the individual if he/she doesn't meet the others expectations.

Example I
The Facilitator/teacher says to Mary, who is painting at the easel, "Mary, today you have taken time and worked hard to get your painting exactly as you want it."

Example II
Andrew, who usually must be reminded to hang up his coat, heard the teacher say, "Andrew, you walked right in the door just now, straight over to your cubby and hung up your coat. No one reminded you. You did it yourself."

Example III
Haseem asks Lemah, "Stop yelling in my ear. I don't like it." Usually Haseem hit Lemah when she yelled around him. Hearing this, the teacher immediately says, "Haseem, you did the right thing when you used words to tell Lemah to stop yelling in your ear and that you didn't like it. You handled that the right way."

SELF-ENDORSEMENT (Developing Positive Self-Identity)

This curriculum has been developed to enhance the self-identity of young children.

Every Creative and Connected© lesson constantly associates affect, cognition, psychomotor and the mindfullness domains in support of each child's positive development.

It uses the child's natural language-movement-as the modality for connecting the child to him/herself, to others, to nature, to classical music and to love and peace. Songs are used to help reinforce how young children are learning about themselves and how precious they are. Each child's unfolding self-identity will be unique and the activities in this curriculum are developed to honor and respect that uniqueness.

FACILITATORS

The Facilitator/teacher does not model patterns of movement for the children. There will be an occasion or two when you will, at the right moment, initiate and share your own pattern (this curriculum will tell you when). That is not the same thing as modeling.

1. It is the children's self-expression you are facilitating.
2. It is the children's creativity and inner beauty you are accessing.
3. It is the unfolding of the children's self-awareness that you are facilitating.
4. It is administering to the children's emotional pain you are assisting in.

Example IV
    The teacher said to Doug, who seldom stays on task, "Today, Doug, you sat right there matching those cards until you finished all of them. No one told you to finish it. You chose to finish!" Then the teacher would help the child connect to his feelings by asking, "How does that make you feel inside when you choose to finish what you've started?" Child verbally responds.

Example V
    Both Jarrell and Andrew are tugging at the bike, trying to ride it. Jarrell, under similar conditions, hits children. Suddenly Jarrell says, "Let's take turns. You go first." The teacher puts her arm around Jarrell and says, "You used your words just now. You didn't hurt Andrew. You used your words! How does that make you feel inside?"

Example VI
　　Building with Legos, Lemah and Jarrell had created an impressive structure. They said, "Teacher, look at our structure." The teacher responded, "I've been watching you. For 20 minutes you have been working together to build that structure, especially to get the top part to stay up and not fall over. And you did it!"

　　When verbally appreciating someone's efforts, describe what is observed. This kind of endorsing (complimenting) is not only freeing, but motivating for life changes. Here is a reminder: When working to modify behavior, it is necessary to keep a written record of how often the unacceptable behavior occurs, so the teacher can chart the child's progress.

　　Note to Facilitators/teachers: We, the developers, feel strongly-as we honor all children-that we make an effort not to make any judgments about the situation, or the reasons why things are happening the way they are happening in a child's life, especially if they are at-risk

FOR THREE-YEAR OLDS

When using a self-endorsement/exploration lesson with three-year old children, make the following change. Have no more than six three-year olds in one class.

In Lesson Six, under "Gallop," do not have three-year olds gallop backward. Usually they have not yet developed the muscle coordination for this.

Do not use the coping skills the first time through Cycle One except for Lesson Seven, and coping skills for scared feelings (bad dreams).

In Lesson Eleven under Emotional Feeling, substitute Lesson Ten Emotional Feeling, then improvise.

When the three-year olds complete Cycle One, repeat it from the beginning and add Lesson Seven coping skills for "sad" only, Lesson Eight coping skills, Lesson Nine coping skills, and Lesson Ten coping skills.

Because Facilitators and children may move through some lessons a little slower than indicated, use the following guidelines, if it becomes necessary to make two lessons out of one lesson. Lessons should not exceed 25 to 30 minutes for three-year olds.

End lesson with improvisation, then sing, "I'm My Friend."

Begin the next lesson by singing, "There's Just One Little Nose" and continue where you left off, then finish class.

WHAT EACH LESSON INCLUDES

Purpose for Each Lesson: To see more of the Why's for each lesson, a page at the beginning of each lesson gives a specific purpose. As you have seen, it is suggested by the author, creator, and researcher of the original work, the lessons are meant to be done in a particular order and in a particular way. The reason for this is the cumulative effect of what is gained by each child from each lesson. The Purpose, then, may help make this order and organization more clear and meaningful. If you've done the lessons, you can see the positive effect they have. If you review the Purpose for each lesson you will know why!

Brain Connections: As mentioned and our examples show, there are specific items on how each lesson may influence brain development. You need to know that science is making daily discoveries in this area. By the time you've done the lessons in this book, many more studies on the brain will have been completed. What we are doing here is providing a link between current studies and brain development, especially for children in stressful situations. Although these lessons are absolutely worthwhile for any child, we have seen real success, real results from children coming from more stressful situations.

So you'll know for your own peace of mind, we make no judgments about the situation or the reasons why things are happening the way they are happening in a child's life. Joni had a child, first or second grader, come to my class one day; he'd hung around before. I knew he liked the atmosphere, but this day he was there much more than was usual. Eventually I heard the story:

The family was living without electricity. They had been lighting the house by burning candles in birdcages. The night before, this child had knocked over a birdcage. The house had burned to the ground. How do you help a child who doesn't even know where to go home that afternoon, or if they will want him if he does? That's stress hitting every fiber of his brain and body. No judgments. Just how can we help a child who needs support and nurturing to grow up to be okay? That's what the philosophy, lessons, and the brain pieces are for. This child-and others like him-are why I continue to study the brain and do the work I do.

MATERIALS NEEDED FOR LESSONS THAT FOLLOW:

Most lessons include music which is listed at the beginning of each lesson. All of these pieces are available on the Internet and easily downloadable for play. You may download them at our website http//www.creativeandconnectedchildren.com. You also have a first lesson-Facilitator video, so you can see how this works.

Music:

Some lessons include specific items. Please note those before you go to class. You will find just the right leaves, flower, and shells for the area you live in. And even better, what you find and use will be easily recognizable by the children. For the shells and crystals, the Michaels stores carry them both in the store and online. We suggest getting them early so you aren't scrambling at the last minute. Items include:

- Real leaves--both big and little
- Beautifully wrapped box--within is a big shell and a little shell
- Real flower--big and little (when the concept of size is repeated, use a different flower such as roses or daisies)
- Shells
- Crystals
- Book: Private Zone by Frances Dayee is available through Amazon and Abe's Books
- Space & Music

Pictures--Several of the lessons include pictures and music and we have these available for download on our website:

www.creativeandconnectedchildren.com/book-resources

The Facilitator Decides the Number of Times a Particular Lesson Needs to be Taught.

For instance lesson one may be taught five times in a row before teaching Lesson Two.

Repeating a lesson helps children have another opportunity to work with the material. Remember: repetition is the first law of learning.

LESSON ONE

By the end of this lesson, the children will be able to do the following:

1. Begin developing a sensitivity to his/her own uniqueness and significance, by singing the self-awareness songs at the beginning and the end of each of the lessons.

2. Engage the first two steps of the creative process with clapping, jumping, and arm patterns.

3. Become aware that she/he can use her/his own movement vocabulary for self-expression.

4. Identify body parts.

5. Demonstrate his/her knowledge of the concept of slow (tempo), by walking slowly (kinesthetic modality).
   a. Begin connecting to the world he/she lives in by identifying animals that walk slowly.

6. Begin developing self-trust by improvising (improvisation means the child dances to the music any way he/she chooses).

PURPOSES FOR LESSON ONE

1. Children with little or no self-awareness have no understanding of their own significance, or how unique they are. Children have their self-awareness reinforced. Facilitators encourage each child to actually sing the songs in the lesson. In actually singing these songs, the message is eventually internalized. Sing these songs during the regular pre-school day as well.

Brain Connections: What happens in the brain when you sing? When you think, your brain is at work and the brain releases chemicals. Some of them are healthy, joyous chemicals. Others are more toxic. When singing, endorphins-a chemical associated with pleasure-and oxytocin-a chemical which alleviates stress-are released. The more a child sings happy songs, the more happy chemicals are released.

2. When a child gets in touch with his/her own creativity, the self-worth is immediately triggered. The child begins to tap into his creative ability through a vital channel, thus enhancing his/her self-worth.

Brain Connections: Creativity comes from parts of the brain working together that don't always work together. When children practice these connections at a young age, they are more likely to work together as children get older. They also can "feel" their success as they create something new. For example, my son Christopher plays the guitar. The more he played, the better he felt.

3. When the child gets in touch with his/her own creativity through the child's natural language-movement-and is provided with the opportunity to use this movement to express himself/herself, the child experiences joy. What happens in the brain?

Brain Connections: Music and movement are the basis for the creative parts of the brain. Music hits one part of the brain. Movement hits another part. Together they engage creativity.

4. It is reassuring to any child to know and be comfortable with his own body. This is part of learning self-respect. What happens in the brain?

Brain Connections: Young children who are encouraged to sing and move in the ways described in this curriculum are sure of their own bodies and naturally more spontaneous. It's like Christopher practicing his guitar. Singing and movement are not the only things that cause a child to be sure of his/her own body but are an impact on the brain.

5. The tempo concept (fast and slow) is part of the child's life. Being able to consciously apply this concept gives the child a feeling of being in control - an unusual feeling for these children. Children then add to their cognitive store.

Brain Connections: Two types of feelings can occur. What we might consider exterior feelings which are registered in the prefrontal cortex of our brain, and interior or inner feelings which are found in more buried middle parts of our brain. Getting to these inner feelings is vital and essential for development.

6. Some children have been taught not to trust. Three dysfunctional rules "taught" in substance-abuse homes are: We don't feel, we don't trust, and we don't talk about real issues. Practice of some of these rules goes on in homes where there is no substance abuse, so children are in dire need of valid opportunities to build self-trust. Through movement, the child's natural language, and through music that reaches his heart, the child begins his/her journey toward self-trust. Children use improvisation for self-expression.

Brain Connections: Improvisation studies show a disconnect between the prefrontal cortex (the thinking part of the brain) and more activity in the inner parts of the brain, perhaps allowing for more self-expression. I use the word "perhaps" because there are so many connections and interactions in the brain, it's difficult to say precisely, but our experience with preschoolers shows a connection between improvisation with music and movement and increased self-expression and inner awareness.

LESSON ONE

SONG:
Facilitator and children sit in a circle on the floor. Facilitator says, "Children, we are going to sing a song about you, about how special you are." All sing, "There's Just One Little Nose Like Mine." Sing with music.

Facilitator and children sit on a floor in a circle. Facilitator says, "We are going to do some things three-, four-, and five-year-olds do so well, like clapping, jumping, and running."

CLAPPING:
Facilitator begins clapping his/her hands (in front of tummy) and sings or chants, "We're clapping our hands, we're clapping our hands, we're clapping our hands." Facilitator stops and says, "We've been clapping our hands like this (and demonstrates). What is another way we can clap our hands?" If no response, the Facilitator repeats the question. If no response still, the Facilitator repeats the statement. "We've been clapping our hands in front of our tummies (and demonstrates). Let's find a different way to clap our hands." As soon as a child responds, the Facilitator repeats the child's clapping pattern and chants, "We're clapping on our knees (or whatever) with Mario's pattern." Do this two times. Repeat original question, "What is a different way to clap our hands?" until all who desire have had a turn. Facilitator endorses, "You found lots of different ways to clap your hands."

RUNNING: (Music is Flight of the Bumblebee by Rimsky-Korsakov)
This will help experience exhilaration, and to use big muscles. Facilitator says, "Run in a circle until the music stops. When the music stops, you stop." The Facilitator puts on the music for about five or six seconds. Smiling, the Facilitator repeats instructions: "Run 'til the music stops." Do this four or five times. (NOTE: If the room is small, Facilitator will need to divide the class in half.) Facilitator and children sit in circle on floor. Facilitator asks each child individually, "Did you like running today?" Child verbally responds.

BODY AWARENESS:
Facilitator can make this fun by covering his/her eyes and saying, "When I open my eyes, children, be touching your nose (repeat same procedure for head, foot, tummy, knees, and arms). Facilitator endorses group. For example, "You did it, children. You did it."

ARM PATTERNS: (music is Liberstraume by Liszt)
Facilitator asks children to, "Show me your arms." Children respond. Facilitator says, "I am going to put on some music and you find ways to move your arms."

Facilitator encourages by commenting, "Naquita's arms are moving, Mary's arms are moving," including each child. When music stops, Facilitator asks children to, "Find a place to stand where no one else is." Facilitator asks children, "Have another turn, children, to let your arms move. Remember, only your arms move. I'll put on the music." To encourage, Facilitator will again make comments like, "There goes Mario's arm pattern. Jerrell's arms are moving." Children and Facilitator will sit on floor. The Facilitator will ask each child, "How did it feel to move your arms to the music?" Children verbally respond.

CONNECTEDNESS:

"Children, do you like your arms?" Children respond. Facilitator asks, "I'm happy we have arms. Aren't you?" the Facilitator comments. Children verbally respond.

SHOW:

Facilitator says "Three-, four- and five-years olds love to jump." Immediately the Facilitator begins clapping his/her hands to provide an accompaniment.

DISCUSS:

Facilitator chants, "Jump, jump, jumping."

APPLY:

Children jump to hand clapping and chanting accompaniment. They do this for 10 seconds. Children sit on floor. Facilitator endorses. For example, "You were jumping today, children."

EXPLORE JUMPING:

The Facilitator then elicits exploring by asking the children to find another way to jump. All the children stand and the Facilitator again provides the same rhythm background by clapping his/her hands. Now the Facilitator begins to describe what she/he sees, such as, "I see jumping fast, I see jumping turning," etc. After six or seven seconds the Facilitator asks the children to lie down on the floor to rest. Quietly, she/he says, "You found different ways to jump, didn't you."

TEMPO:

Children and Facilitator sit in circle on the floor.

SHOW:

Facilitator shows a picture of an elephant.

DISCUSS:
Facilitator asks, "Do elephants walk fast or slowly?" Children verbally respond. Facilitator will correct any child who gives a wrong response.

APPLY:
The Facilitator asks the children to walk slowly. As children comply, Facilitator remarks, "Jarrell is walking so slowly, Lemah is walking so slowly." Each child is mentioned. If a child is walking too fast, Facilitator says, "Mario, walk slowly."

CONNECTEDNESS:
Facilitator asks, "What else moves slowly besides an elephant?" Children verbally respond.

IMPROVISATION: (music is Fur Elise by Beethoven)
Children and Facilitator sit in a circle on the floor. Facilitator comments, "Children, you are such thinkers today." As she/he puts on the music, the Facilitator says, "I will put on the music and you can dance any way you want to." To the first child who gets up, the Facilitator says, "There goes Haseem. There goes Andrew," etc. Facilitator comments while the children are dancing, "You are dancing, children!" Facilitator and children sit on the floor. Facilitator asks each child, "How did you like dancing to the music?" Children verbally respond.

CLOSURE:
Facilitator endorses each child. For example, "Lemah, I liked the way you took your turn each time, today. Haseem, I'm so happy you decided to follow the rules so you could stay in our class. Mario, you found lots of ways to move your arms, didn't you?"

SONG:
Facilitator says, "We're going to sing another song that says you are your own friend." All sing, "I'm My Friend." Sing with music.

LESSON TWO

By the end of this lesson the children will be able to do the following:

1. Sing the two self-worth awareness songs.

2. Explore different ways to clap and add one or two more ideas.

3. Run until music stops, then stop themselves by dropping to the floor.

4. Identify their body parts (arm, leg, ear, foot, and nose) by touching as Facilitator indicates.

5. Find ways to move their arms, with some children finding a different arm pattern than used in Lesson One.

6. Explore different ways to jump.

7. Apply the concept of "slow" to two other parts of their bodies (heads, legs), then select from four pictures things that move slowly.

8. Freeze, or stop in a special way, when Facilitator indicates.

9. Improvise or dance to the music, in their own way.

PURPOSE FOR LESSON TWO

1. Singing these songs is encouraging to children.

Brain Connections: What happens in the brain when each of these areas is activated—singing, movement? Choral singing has been found to have positive effects. It raises the "happy" chemicals—as well as lowering the stress chemical of cortisol. Movement is connected to learning in the cerebellum.

2. 2,5,6,8, and 9. In Lesson Two, the children are engaging the first three steps in the creative process with becoming aware, exploring and improvising. Becoming aware of his/her own creativity and immediately applying it triggers self-confidence. Being able to perceive a concept (slow) and successfully apply it (answer the question, "What moves slowly besides an elephant?") helps the child feel he/she can achieve. When given a pattern for relating to the concept, the child finds meaning or relevance.

Brain Connections: Another important brain chemical is dopamine. Oddly enough, dopamine often arrives in the anticipation of an achievement. When a child can see and then anticipate that a concept has meaning for him/her, there's a chemical release that "feels" good. Experiencing this feeling is something we want for developing neural pathways. Answering questions correctly connects the child with the happy chemical, dopamine.

3. Alternating using big muscles, then using small muscles, not only relaxes, but assists accomplishment. How does this affect a child's brain?

Brain Connections: Movement means the cells need to work together in the body. When the cells in big and small muscles communicate, they do so through the release of dopamine. Dopamine is one of those "feel good" chemicals. It's another reason to move the muscles and then relax them.

4. Being able to identify body parts is a way of becoming aware of self.

Brain Connections: There are three areas of the brain that are major contributors to one's self awareness. These include the insular cortex, the anterior cingulate cortex, and the medial prefrontal cortex. The motor cortex lies behind the prefrontal cortex and is where movement is coordinated. Movement of the different body parts assists a child in being aware, not only of his/her body, but of the inner self.

5. If a child can apply a concept with different parts of his/her body, the child is internalizing the concept. What happens in the brain?

Brain Connections: Becoming aware of the inner self helps in moving the body and activating its parts.

6. Improvisation develops spontaneity. At-risk children lack spontaneity, probably because it requires self-trust. Life has little joy without some spontaneity. Children use improvisation to express themselves, causing them to feel joy.

Brain Connections: There is a place in the middle of the brain called the amygdala. You'll hear about the amygdala a good deal in these boxes. The amygdala is considered to be the place in the brain where fear is activated. When the amygdala is engaged, say when you are frightened by a snake, the brain goes to one of three responses: fight, flight, or freeze. The diagram on the next page provides a look at the amygdala and the hypothalamus where many memories are stored.
Because the amygdala connects with the strongest memories, it can also connect to joy. Having more joyful memories than fearful ones help in the expression of joy. Facilitators/teachers can help create those joyful experiences with a child.

7. Begin uncloaking a child's feelings. Because at-risk children have not been able to talk about feelings, this curriculum provides constant opportunity. Talking about feelings is surely necessary for achieving wholeness.

Brain Connections: Children who are at-risk and lack self-trust are coming from stress and fear much more often than other children. Their amygdala is activated much more often from fear. Improvisation allows them a safe place to be spontaneous and to feel joy. Their initial trials may seem very subdued or quite wild, but with practice they can learn to trust their own spontaneity. I taught Special Ed for a number of years. One day a third grade teacher called me and through gritted teeth said, "Come get this kid." I didn't need to ask who. I just went to her class and asked him if he wanted to come help me. He stopped his activities and came to help.

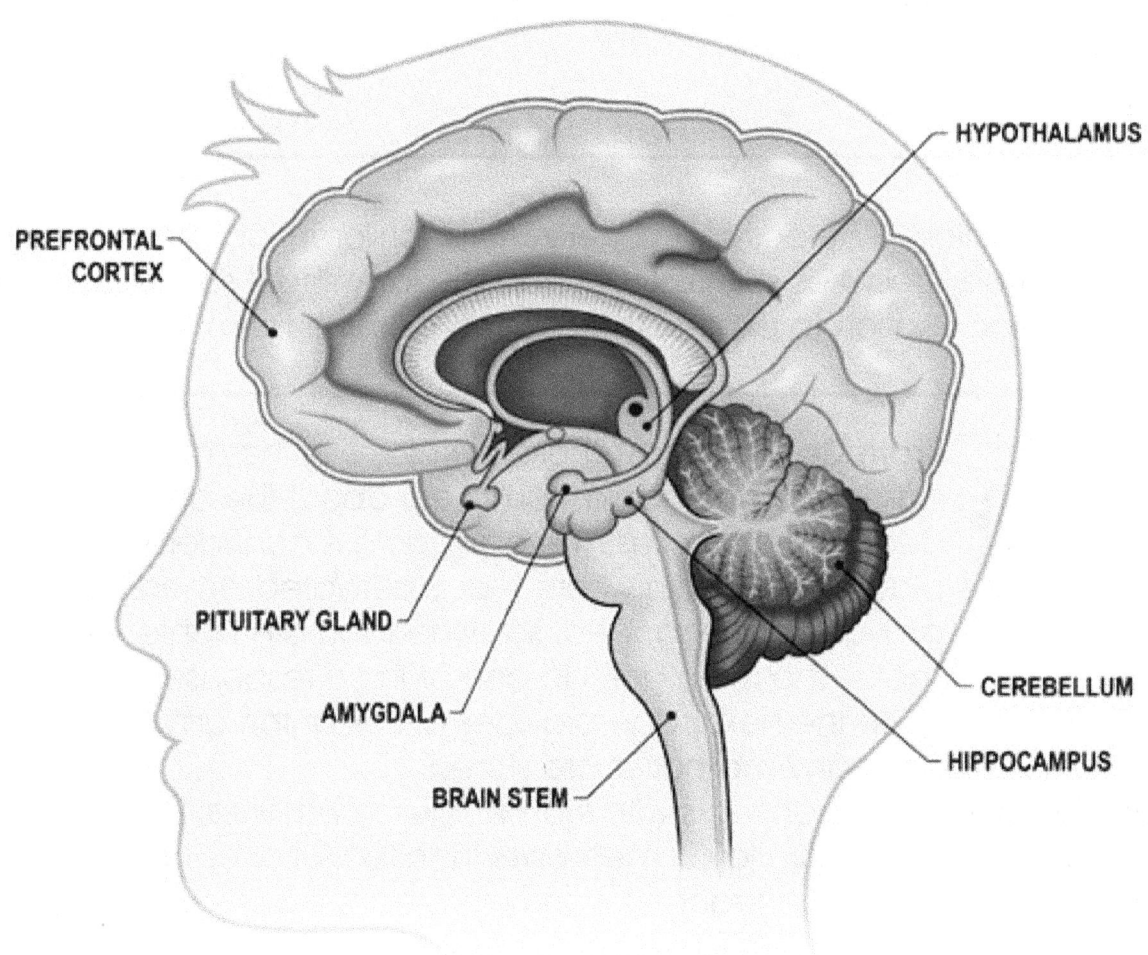

LESSON TWO

SONG:
Facilitator and children sit on floor in a circle. All sing, "There's Just One Little Nose Like Mine." Sing with music.

CLAP:
Facilitator asks the children, "What's another way to clap our hands?" As soon as a child responds, Facilitator says, "We're clapping our hands with Lemah's pattern." Facilitator repeats procedure with each child. If no new patterns are forthcoming, that is, the children only repeated patterns from the last class, the Facilitator says, "Today, we've clapped our hands (describe what children did). Now, let's find a different way to clap our hands." Do two or three of the children's new patterns. Facilitator recognizes their efforts by endorsing. For examples, the Facilitator says, "You did it. You found different clapping patterns!" Facilitator asks children, "Do you like to clap?" Children verbally respond.

RUN: (music is Flight of the Bumble Bee by R. Korsakov)
The Facilitator says "Children, if you like to run, touch your nose." Children respond. Facilitator says, "You are going to run in a circle, and stop as soon as the music stops." Half of the class of children will remain seated by Facilitator, while the other half stands in a big circle. The Facilitator asks the children who are standing, "When the music stops, what will you do, children?" (Stop down on the floor). The Facilitator puts on the music. Children respond. The music stops, children drop on the floor and stop. Repeat twice more. Facilitator makes an encouraging comment such as, "You did it! The moment that music stopped, you stopped down on the floor!" This half of the class sits down, and the other half stands in a big circle to have a turn. The Facilitator repeats the procedure.

BODY AWARENESS:
Children and Facilitator are seated on floor in a circle. Facilitator will cover his/her eyes, and say, "When I open my eyes, be touching your ear." Children respond. Facilitator uncovers eyes and quickly checks each child. Facilitator covers his/her eyes and says, "When I open my eyes, be touching your chin." Children respond. Facilitator follows same procedure, having children touch their toes, shoulders, eyes, thumbs, and arms. Facilitator endorses.

ARMS: (Music is Opus 32 by Brahms)
Children and Facilitator are seated on floor in circle. Facilitator reminds children that, "You found some ways to move your arms last time. Find some ways to move your arms today." Facilitator puts on music. Facilitator encourages by commenting on any child who begins. For example, "Naquita's found a way to move her arms. Mario's found a way to move his arms." As soon as music stops,

Facilitator asks the children to find a space to stand in. The Facilitator might say, "Your ideas are coming, aren't they? Go find a space to stand to do your arm patterns. Remember, children, only your arms move." Facilitator puts on the music. Children respond. Facilitator describes what he/she sees. When all the children have finished, the children sit on the floor and Facilitator asks, "Do you like to use your arms, children?" Children verbally respond.

JUMP:

The Facilitator, while clapping his/her hands says, "Go and jump, children." The Facilitator, while clapping, chants or sings (use any tune):

"Jump, jump, jumping,
Jump, jump, jumping,
We love to jump."

Do this for approximately twenty seconds. Facilitator says, "Stop." Children respond. Facilitator endorses (for example: Facilitator could describe what he/she saw). Children sit on floor in a circle.

EXPLORE JUMPING:

Facilitator says, "All right, children, what's another way to jump?" If no one responds, Facilitator can say, "You've been jumping in one spot; find another way to jump." The moment a child jumps differently, start describing what is seen. For example, "Mary's turning while she jumps. Lemah's arms are helping her jump, Andrew's jumping backward."

Children return to sit in circle on the floor. Facilitator endorses. For example, "You found lots of ways to jump, didn't you?" Facilitator asks each child, "How do you feel about jumping today?" Children verbally respond.

SHOW:

Facilitator walks slowly.

DISCUSS:

Facilitator asks: "Children, am I walking slow or fast?" children respond. Correct any wrong answers.

APPLY 1:

Facilitator says, "Now you walk slowly." Children respond. Facilitator endorses. (For example: Facilitator says, "You walked so slowly.")

APPLY 2:

Facilitator says, "Show me what other part of your body besides your feet you can move slowly." Children respond. If children don't respond, Facilitator says, "Move your head slowly." Children respond. Facilitator says, "Move your leg slowly." Facilitator endorses. Facilitator asks, "Do you like to move slowly?" Children respond.

APPLY 3:

Facilitator shows children two pictures and says, "Tell me which moves slowly." (turtle, rabbit) Correct any wrong choices. Facilitator endorses.

FREEZE:

Facilitator says, "I'm going to teach you something that's fun! I'm going to teach you how to do a freeze. Stand in a place where no one else is." Children respond. Facilitator says, "A freeze means to stop, but it means to stop in a special way. Children, do a freeze, or stop, with <u>one hand in the air</u>." Children respond. Facilitator endorses. For example, "You <u>are</u> doing a freeze with one hand in the air." Facilitator says, "Children, do a different freeze with one hand on the floor." Facilitator endorses. Facilitator says, "Do a freeze on your knees." Children respond. Facilitator endorses. Facilitator says, "Now, children, do a freeze any way you want to." When all are in a freeze, Facilitator endorses. For example, "Look at those freezes!"

IMPROVISATION: (music is Waltz of the Flowers by Tchaikovsky)

Facilitator says, "You have lots of ideas today, children. I brought some beautiful music for you to dance to." Facilitator puts on music. Facilitator says, "Find a space, children, and dance your own way." The moment a child starts to dance, the Facilitator encourages by saying, "There goes Jarrell. There goes Mario." When the music stops, the Facilitator says, "Freeze!" When all the children are in a freeze, the Facilitator says, "Thank you." (NOTE: Unless there is ample room, divide the class in half for improvisation.) Children sit in a circle on the floor. The Facilitator asks each child, "Did you like dancing to the music today?" Child verbally responds.

CLOSURE:

Facilitator endorses group. For example, the Facilitator might say, "Children, you are finding out you have lots of ideas inside you, aren't you?" Facilitator endorses self. For example, "I think I did a good job helping you today."

SONG:

All sing with music "I'm My Friend."

LESSON THREE

By the end of this lesson, the children will be able to do the following:

1. Sing more words of the self-worth songs (especially if these songs are being sung several times each week during other parts of the pre-school day.

2. Run with arms helping, and freeze when music stops.

3. Find ways to move their arms, then share one of their arm patterns with each other.

4. Use the tempo (slow) concept with their arms, and become aware of how tempo relates to the world they live in.

5. Apply the tempo concept (fast) by walking and moving their arms fast.

6. Relate the tempo concept to themselves.

7. Apply the second step of the creative process (exploring) while jumping.

8. Each child will tell how he/she feels about doing it.

9. Relate to each other by touching thumbs.

10. Identify the emotional feeling of sad

11. By looking at a picture of a sad child; each child will talk about when he/she feels sad; and apply that feeling by walking sadly.

12. Become aware of relating feeling to others (connectedness) by listening to a question and responding.

13. Improvise to the music.

14. Listen to the Facilitator endorse the group.

PURPOSES FOR LESSON THREE

1. Each time the children sing the self-worth songs, the music carries the message to their hearts, "I am of worth." What happens in the brain?

Brain Connections: In the first lesson we mentioned the release of chemicals in the brain when you sing. That continues here, just look and listen to the words in the songs. Both are about each child as a special being. "One Little Nose Like Mine" is about the uniqueness of the child. "I'm My Friend" reinforces who I am. These songs sung over and over help build the neuronal pathways in the brain and reminders of their own specialness.

2. The careful sequence of increasing movement vocabulary assures the child's success. Follow this curriculum book carefully.

Brain Connections: There are two areas on the left side of the brain involved in language development—the Broca and Wernicke areas. Vocabulary and self-expression are things that will help not only the brain development, but a child's self-trust. Repetition aides learning and the developing neural pathways. Repeating the movements in a consistent order helps a child to feel safe and ready to grow.

3. Having peers try out the child's creative efforts (child's ideas) gives the message "You have a worthwhile idea" in a powerful way.

Brain Connections: We characterize the brain as having a left and right hemisphere, and the two work together. On both sides there is a superior temporal gyrus. This is where we find creativity. The left side has short dendroids or branches for pulling in nearby information. The right side has longer branches reaching into distant parts of the brain. Those branches can bring a new idea. An "aha" moment is not only fun, but when reinforced, children want to do it again as others recognize their effort.

4. Being able to apply the tempo concept in new ways increases feelings of being in control, and increases the capacity to use a concept in new ways.

Brain Connections: If you consistently use the same vocabulary and movement—practice those—neurons will be retained rather than pruned or lost. Again the more practice, the more skill and self trust is developed.

5. The child is given opportunity and encouragement to talk about his/her feelings. Remember, the message they've been taught is "don't feel." We slowly begin reconnecting the child to his/her feelings.

Brain Connections: Getting to feelings-real feelings beyond just the fear-is very important for a child's neural development. Having them identify their feelings is a major step in knowing how to stay safe and for all children to be who they really are—whole and complete and connected to the Spiritual.

6. Touching thumbs is a gentle, non-threatening way to physically relate to a peer. For children it's fun. For the child whose circles of connectedness are shattered, it is significant.

Brain Connections: In yoga the thumb represents universal consciousness. There is also a closed connection to the brain when the index finger and the thumb touch. Perhaps thumb touching helps close the circuit for a child.

7. Recognizing and identifying feeling, then being able to apply the feeling, is part of reconnecting the child to his/her feelings.

Brain Connections: Have you checked in with your own feelings? These activities may be bringing up issues for you. Know that you may be developing new neural pathways as well as the children. Neuroplasticity is alive, well, and at work for everyone-- including the adults working with children.

8. Improvising to classical music allows the child to get in touch with the inner self, to learn self-trust, and provides an authentic experience for expressing him/herself. This is just as valid for all children.

Brain Connections: There seems to be a correlation between listening to classical music and dopamine production. As a reminder, dopamine is one of the brain's feel-good chemicals. In our experience classical music is much more likely to produce the desired self-trust and improvisation we desire than is more modern music. What we are looking for here is a child experiencing his/her authentic self, which is more apparent with the classical music. Leigh tells a story of a mom of one of her preschoolers telling her about she and her child hearing some music one day and the child said, "That's Mrs. Shannon's music."

9. All children's confidence is expanded when an adult, in a supervising role, verbally recognizes their efforts.

Brain Connections: Words are very important in these lessons. We as adults or children are used to others telling us what we think, how we should do things, what's right, and especially how we feel. Our brain gets very used to this outside direction. In these activities, we are asking children to discover their inside directions. Infancy and preschool are the years in which we are conditioned by the adults around us to listen to them. In the process, children may lose the ability to listen to themselves. These lessons give them the opportunity to tune in to their inner selves. Recognize and encourage them when they do so!

LESSON THREE

SONG:
Facilitator and children are sitting on floor in a circle. Facilitator says, "Let's sing that song that tells how special you are." All sing "There's Just One Little Nose Like Mine." Sing with music.

Facilitator:
"Are you ready to do some things that three-, four-, and five-year olds do so well?"

RUNNING:
Arms Helping (Music, Flight of the Bumble Bee by Rimsky-Korsakov) Facilitator says, "Today you will run until the music stops, and then when the music stops, you will freeze. Let your arms help while you are running." As the children run, Facilitator may need to remind by recognizing children whose arms are helping as they run. If some children do not use their arms as they run, have all sit in circle, discuss it, and give those children who did not use their arms another turn to run with arms helping. Facilitator endorses those children. Facilitator asks each child in the class, "How did it feel to have your arms helping as you ran?"

ARM PATTERNS:
Try out each other's patterns (Music, Waltz in A-Flat, Opus 39 by Brahms Facilitator might say, "Children, you've been finding ways to move your arms. Today, find a different way for your arms to move." Music is put on as children find their own space in which to stand. The Facilitator responds as in previous lessons, "Haseem is moving his arms," etc.

Facilitator says, "Today, your arm patterns need to be shared! Each child may have a turn to share your arm pattern with the rest of the children." And immediately the music is turned on, and the Facilitator asks a specific child to do his/her pattern. This continues until each child who desires to do so has had a turn to share his/her arm patterns with the class. For example, "Mary, share your arm pattern. Mary's arm pattern goes around. Jarrell's trying Mary's arm pattern. Everyone do Mary's arm pattern." Facilitator asks, "Did you like sharing your arm patterns today, children?" Children respond.

TEMPO:
Children and Facilitator sit in a circle on the floor. Facilitator says, "Watch me."

SHOW:
Facilitator stands and walks slowly.

DISCUSS:
"Am I walking fast or slow?" the Facilitator asks. Children verbally respond. Then Facilitator asks, "Remember how slowly you walked last class?" Facilitator sits on floor and asks children to:

Apply #1:
"Walk slowly." Children respond. Facilitator comments: "You are walking slowly."

Apply #2:
Children and Facilitator sit on floor, and Facilitator asks children to move their arms slowly. Facilitator makes encouraging comments.

CONNECTEDNESS:
Facilitator says, "I'm glad we can move slowly and we can move fast anytime we need to!" Facilitator asks the class, "Do you feel glad we can move fast or slow anytime we need to?" Children verbally respond.

JUMPING:
Facilitator says, "You three-, four-, and five-year-old children are jumpers!

AWARE:
Immediately the Facilitator begins clapping her/his hands for background accompaniment and says.

EXPLORE:
"Could you jump forward?" Children respond. "Could you jump backward?" Children respond. "Could you jump turning?" Children respond. "Could you jump any way?" Children respond.

IMPROVISE:
The Facilitator says, "Go find you own space to jump," while continuing to clap to the background accompaniment. Facilitator describes what she/he sees, such as, "I see jumping turning. I see arms helping jump. I see jumping on one foot." The children jump for several seconds.
Children return to circle and sit on the floor. The Facilitator says, "You found lots of different ways to jump!" The Facilitator asks each child, "Did you like finding different ways to jump today?"

CONNECTEDNESS:
Facilitator asks, "What animals can jump?" Children respond.

BODY AWARENESS:
Facilitator covers his/her eyes in playful attitude and says, "When I open my eyes, be touching your heels." Facilitator opens eyes and checks. Correct any mistakes! Repeat procedure with baby toe, chin, thumb, leg. Facilitator chooses specific children to sit in front of other children, who would be compatible. For example, "Haseem, sit in front of Naquita please." When each child is sitting in front of a partner, Facilitator asks children to, "Touch your thumb to your partner's thumb." Facilitator endorses. Facilitator asks children, "Touch your other thumb to your partner's thumb." Do three times in all. Facilitator asks, "Was it fun to touch your partner's thumbs, children?" Children verbally respond.

GALLOP:
The Facilitator says to the children, "Find your own space and go galloping." The Facilitator begins clapping an accented rhythm (clap CLAP clap CLAP) while chanting, "Gallop like a little horse, gallop like a little horse." Do this for seven or eight seconds, then children come back and sit in the circle. Facilitator chooses half of the class to have a turn, then the other half, always using endorsing comments such as, "You did it!" Facilitator asks the class, "Did you like galloping today?"

EMOTIONAL FEELING: (No musical accompaniment)
Facilitator says, "We are going to talk about emotional feelings--that means the feelings we have inside ourselves like happy, sad, or mad."

SHOW:
Facilitator shows picture of a sad child.

DISCUSS:
Facilitator asks, "What is this child feeling?" If no response, have each child look at picture, then repeat the question.

Facilitator asks each child, "What makes you feel sad, Naquita?" Child verbally responds. It is possible a child will make a response that is unrelated to a sad feeling. If so, the Facilitator can kindly say, "Right now we are talking about sad feelings. What makes you feel sad, Mario?" As each child responds, the Facilitator may want to say, "That made you sad," or "That is sad."

APPLY:
Facilitator will say, "Children, I want to see you do a sad walk." As the children respond, the Facilitator will endorse by saying, "Lemah's so sad. Mary's sad. Andrew's doing a sad walk." Children return to sit on floor by the Facilitator, she/he can reinforce by saying, "Children, you were so sad."

CONNECTEDNESS:
Facilitator asks a rhetorical question, "Does everyone have feelings? Yes! Everyone has feelings."

IMPROVISE: (Music, Tales of Vienna Woods by Strauss)
Facilitator says, "I'm putting on some music I think you may like. Go and find your own space, and dance your own way." Music is immediately played and Facilitator says, "Naquita's dancing. Haseems's dancing," etc. If children are crowded, have four children at a time improvise. When the music stops, the children freeze until Facilitator says, "Thank you." Children sit in a circle on floor. Facilitator asks each child, "Did you like dancing today?

CLOSURE:
Facilitator makes group endorsement. For example, Facilitator says "Children, I liked the way you really worked today with the sad feelings." Facilitator pauses for a second (to shift to self) and does self-endorsement. For example, "And I liked the way I had all the music ready for our class today."

SONG:
Facilitator and children sing, "I'm My Friend." Sing with music.

LESSON FOUR

By the end of lesson Four, the children will be able to do the following:

1. Sing self-worth song, "There's Just One Little Nose Like Mine."

2. Find different ways to clap.

3. Run to the music while holding their arms in different freezes.

4. Lift their legs front and back, then explore other ways to do leg lifts.

5. Answer connectedness questions.

6. Body awareness facing a partner.

7. Share arm patterns.

8. Work with the concept of tempo.

9. Gallop using arms.

10. Look at a picture and identify feeling.

11. Use direction.

12. Improvise.

PURPOSES FOR LESSON FOUR

1. Singing the self-worth songs helps children to take the message of the song into their hearts and minds. What happens in the brain?

Brain Connections: Just another reminder about how much singing connects a child to himself and others. The songs also include practicing the words and feelings his/her brain need to reinforce.

2. Following these lessons carefully assures the child's success with his/her movement vocabulary.

Brain Connections: The second brain center for movement is the cerebellum. It doesn't originate movement, but it coordinates the movement between the brain and the body.

3. Running has exhilarative value.

Brain Connections: When the brain (thought) and body (movement) connect, there is a feeling of progress, action and joy that isn't found in many other activities.

4. Exploring leg lifts increases the child's creativity.

Brain Connections: It's the exploring new ideas and ways to do things (thought) that connects with movement and then the "aha" becomes something the child can feel and know.

5. Answering connectedness questions helps the child to link to his/her environment.

Brain Connections: A child usually isn't aware of the environment around his or her. It's like a fish isn't aware it's in water. When we as adults ask questions and explore what the environment is, a child can begin to see other possibilities. Until those possibilities are presented, the child may not even realize the toxicity of the environment he/she is in.

6. Learning body parts helps children to have self-respect.

Brain Connections: If you don't like your body or parts of your body, it's hard to have good thoughts about who you are. Learning to care for ourselves includes appreciating all of who we are. I've mentioned one of my sons. When he was little he had what is called Perthes leg. It required him to wear a brace for months. He could easily have hated the brace and his not working hip joint. He didn't. He, and we, made the best of it, and he is currently running a medical clinic in the Air Force. Seems he has overcome whatever issues in both body and brain.

7. Sharing each other's patterns builds self-confidence mightily.

Brain Connections: Chemicals are released in the brain when events occur. When someone else uses your patterns, or acts on your suggestions, a number of "happy" chemicals are released in the system. A child can "feel" the results.

8. Being able to apply the tempo concept in new ways, again increases the child's feeling of being in control and increases his capacity to use a concept in new ways.

Brain Connections: Toxic stress weakens the building and developing brain. Giving the brain new and positive ways to think and create helps develop more neural connections for handling all situations without stress.

9. Working with emotional feeling is not only a relief, but freeing for these children who have been taught to deny feeling.

Brain Connections: All young children first connect with feelings since the brain isn't yet developed enough for thought. Denying or negating feelings is like denying or negating the self. A child loses his/her self when he/she loses track of feeling. This curriculum helps to restore feelings that might have been, consciously or unconsciously, denied.

10. Improvising to classical music allows a child to get in touch with his/her inner self, to learn self-trust, and provides an authentic experience for expressing him/herself.

Brain Connections: The Brain connects to authenticity. There seems to be a subconscious connection to someone who is being real. A child and an adult both seem to connect with that realness. As children become more authentic and connect to their own inner being, others are more attracted to them.

LESSON FOUR

SONG:
Facilitator and children are seated on floor in a circle. All sing, "There's Just One Little Nose Like Mine." All sing with music. Facilitator says, "Children, I've been thinking about you, and what hard workers you are! I'm glad you're here today."

CLAP:
Facilitator says, "Children, you are going to find some more new ideas today." Immediately Facilitator begins clapping his/her hands and chanting, "Let's clap our hands," until all are clapping, then Facilitator asks, "What's a different way to clap our hands?" Each child is offered a turn. (Be accepting if a child chooses not to take a turn.) Facilitator endorses. For example, "You did find some new ways to clap today!"

RUN: (Music, Minute Waltz by Chopin)
Facilitator says, "Find your own way to make your arms freeze," while arms hold a freeze. When every child has an arm freeze, Facilitator says, "Keep your arms in your freeze and run to the music." Facilitator repeats, "Hold your arm freeze as long as you are running to the music." And immediately running music is played. When the music stops, the Facilitator says, "Freeze." The Facilitator then asks the children to find a different arm freeze, and keep that arm freeze while running. Music is again played and the children run while holding the new arm freeze until music stops. Facilitator says, "Freeze." Children and Facilitator sit on floor. The Facilitator asks children, "Was it hard to keep your arms in a freeze the whole time you ran?" Children verbally respond. Facilitator asks, "Did you like running today?" Children respond. Facilitator can have children take one more turn, if children would like to do so.

LEG LIFTS:
Facilitator says, "Lie down on your back." Children respond. Facilitator says, "Your legs are going to have a turn."

AWARE:
Facilitator claps his/her hands, and chants, "Lift one leg, and put it down. Lift the other leg, and put it down." Do four times on each leg. Children are asked to roll onto their tummies in order to lift the leg to the back. The Facilitator may need to take time to coach a little, and to encourage. Lifting the leg to the back is more difficult. Do four times on each leg, alternating legs.

EXPLORE:
The Facilitator will ask the children, "What is another way to lift your leg besides lying on the floor? Show me." Children respond.

IMPROVISE: (Music, Prelude in C by Bach)
Facilitator puts on music. Again, the Facilitator will describe what she/he sees. "Jarrell is standing up and doing a leg lift. Lemah's arms are helping her do a leg lift. Liza is doing a leg lift to the side," etc. When music stops, Facilitator says, "Freeze" and endorses children. Children sit on the floor in a circle besides Facilitator.

BODY AWARENESS:
Facilitator will select couples to face each other (NOTE: Carefully select children who will be amenable as partners. This is the beginning of helping children to relate to each other.) Facilitator says, "Children, touch your nose." Children respond. Facilitator follows same procedure with chin, knee, back, elbow, and neck. The Facilitator asks each child, "How did you like doing that, facing a partner?" The Facilitator asks children to get another partner and do it again. The Facilitator then asks the children as a class, "Did you like doing that with a partner, children?" Children verbally respond.

ARMS: (Music, Fur Elise by Beethoven)
Facilitator tells children, "You've been getting ideas for patterns today, haven't you?" Facilitator puts on music, and says, "Find your own space and do an arm pattern." Facilitator encourages, "There goes Andrew's arm pattern. There goes Mario's." When children have done an arm pattern, Facilitator stops the children and the music and says, "Children, you have your patterns coming so well, let's share with each other. Naquita, do your arm pattern." And Facilitator immediately starts music. Facilitator says, "Children, do Naquita's arm pattern with her. Do your arms the way she's doing it." (Naquita does her arm pattern three or four times.) Facilitator calls on next child to share his/her arm pattern. All children do that pattern. Facilitator continues until all children have had a turn. Facilitator describes what he/she sees. Children return and sit in a circle on floor.

CONNECTEDNESS:
Facilitator asks, "Children, do you like your arms?" Children verbally responds. Facilitators says, "I like my arms, too."

TEMPO:
The Facilitator says, "We are going to talk about fast and slow again today." Facilitator asks children to, "Go lie down in your own space." Children respond. Facilitator asks children to, "Move your legs so-o s-l-o-w-l-y." Facilitator describes what he/she sees: "Lemah's legs are moving slowly. Andrew's legs are moving so slowly." Facilitator says, "Now move your legs fast, move your legs fast, move your legs fast." Children sit on their seats. Facilitator says, "Move your arms so-o-o s-l-o-w-l-y – Move your arms FAST!" Facilitator says to children, "This next one is not easy, children. Are you ready to try a hard one?" Children respond. Facilitator says,

"Jump s-o-o s-l-o-w-l-y." Facilitator describes what he/she sees. Then Facilitator says, "Jump fast! Jump fast!" Do for two or three seconds. Children sit on floor in a circle. Facilitator endorses. For example, "Children, give yourself a hug for doing hard things today!"

GALLOP:

The Facilitator begins clapping galloping rhythm (clap <u>clap</u>, clap <u>clap</u>) and asks the children to gallop in a circle for five or six seconds. Facilitator stops group and makes encouraging comment. Then she/he asks children to find an arm freeze and "Show it to me." When children have responded, the Facilitator asks children to hold their arm freezes as long as they gallop, and the Facilitator begins the clapping rhythm again (clap <u>clap</u>, clap <u>clap</u>). Do for five seconds. Children return to sit on the floor. The Facilitator asks the children, "How does galloping make you feel?" Children verbally respond. Facilitator asks children, "Lie down on floor to rest." Children rest for about 10 seconds.

EMOTIONAL FEELING:

Children sit in circle. The Facilitator will say, "Last class we talked about feelings we all have inside … like happy feelings … what are some other feelings?" When a child mentions "sad," the Facilitator may say, "Last class you did a sad walk, didn't you?" The Facilitator will tell the children, "Today we are not going to talk about sad feelings."

SHOW:

A picture of a happy child.

DISCUSS:

Facilitator asks, "What is this child feeling?" If no response, Facilitator can say, "What do you think this child is feeling?" Children verbally respond. Facilitator asks, "What do you think could have happened to make this child feel happy?" Facilitator then asks each child, "Mario, what makes you feel happy?"

APPLY:

Facilitator asks the children, "Go stand in your own space and do a happy freeze." If children seem hesitant, the Facilitator may ask the children to sit on the floor while the Facilitator does a freeze that's angry. She/he asks the children, while holding the freeze, "Is this a happy freeze?" (No) The Facilitator comes back to the children and says, "You talked about what makes you happy; go stand in your own space and do a happy freeze." If even one child comes close, the others will come along as the Facilitator says, "Andrew has a happy freeze," etc. Facilitator asks each child, "How did you feel about doing a happy feeling?"

DIRECTION:
Children and Facilitator sit on floor in circle. Facilitator says, "We are going to talk about direction."

SHOW:
Facilitator walks forward (toward children).

DISCUSS:
Facilitator asks, "Children, which direction am I walking?" If children don't respond, Facilitator asks, "Am I walking backward?" Facilitator may need to give children the word, "Forward."

APPLY:
Facilitator sits and asks children to walk forward. Children respond. Facilitator says, "That's right."

SHOW:
Facilitator walks backward.

DISCUSS:
Facilitator asks the children, "Which direction am I walking?" (Backward) Children verbally respond.

APPLY:
Facilitator sits down and asks the children to walk backward. Facilitator gives encouragement as children respond.

SHOW:
Facilitator walks sideways, both to the right and to the left.

DISCUSS:
Facilitator asks, "Which direction am I walking?" Children verbally respond.

APPLY:
Facilitator sits and asks children to walk sideways. Children respond. Facilitator asks children, "Walk sideways the other way." Facilitator encourages.

CONNECTEDNESS:
Children and Facilitator sit on floor in circle. Facilitator asks children, "What if we could not move backward – only forward?" After children are through predicting, Facilitator asks the class, "Would you like that?" Children verbally respond. Facilitator says "I am happy we can move forward, side, and backward." Are you? Children verbally respond.

IMPROVISE: (Music, Tales of the Vienna Woods by Strauss)
Facilitator says, "I am going to put on some music, and you may have a turn to go and dance any way you want to. The music will help you get ideas." Immediately music begins. Children respond. Facilitator can encourage by naming the children who have started to respond. For example, "There goes Lemah. There goes Mario."
Children sit in circle. Facilitator asks each child, "Did you like dancing to the music today?" Child verbally respond.

CLOSURE:
Facilitator does individual endorsement of each child. For example, "I am so impressed, Andrew, with the way you lifted your legs to the back today. You really reached! Naquita, you jumped so slowly!" etc. Do a group endorsement on emotional feeling. Facilitator may say, "Children, it's not always easy to talk about feelings, but you did it!"

SONG:
Facilitator and children sing, "I'm My Friend." Sing with music."

LESSON FIVE

By the end of Lesson Five, the children will be able to do the following:

1. Become more involved in the self-worth songs by learning more of the words.

2. Find his/her own way to freeze when the child's name is called, and holding that freeze until every child has had a turn.

3. Stretch leg muscles. Children will choose a partner and hold partner's hands while stretching.

4. Run while using the direction concepts of forward, backward, and sideways.

5. Share his/her arm pattern with the group and the group does it with the child. Facilitator shares an arm pattern with the children. Facilitator may choose his/her own.

6. Respond to connectedness and feeling questions.

7. Using his/her own arm freeze, gallop using forward and side directions.

8. After viewing a picture of a child, the children in the group will be able to identify the angry feeling of the child in the picture; verbally share one thing that makes each child in the group angry (mad), then do an angry (mad) freeze.

9. Practice three coping skills for angry (mad) feelings.

10. Lift each leg front and to the back. Then, while listening to the music, the children will do leg lifts in their own ways. They will respond to a feeling question.

11. Respond to connectedness question.

12. Explore different ways to turn. Respond to a feeling question.

13. Find his/her own way to dance to the music. Respond to a feeling question.

14. Listen to Facilitator endorse the group and as Facilitator also does self-endorsement.

PURPOSES FOR LESSON FIVE

Remember, making it possible for children to discover their own creativity, the fine and good within, then providing for implementation in a relevant way, through their own "language" or kinesthetic modality, is a direct shot into their self- worth "blood stream," so to speak.

Since at-risk children have learned to stuff down their feelings, talking about feelings, then practicing those feelings are two necessary steps toward wholeness. Children's ability to communicate their feelings with greater clarity is considerably enhanced. Being endorsed appropriately by an adult in charge, and hearing the adult endorse himself/herself, gives hope and the courage to try, to all children. It is also a model for them.

BRAIN CONNECTION: How does what we're doing affect brain development? A recent brain study actually has located a spot in the brain for self-esteem. It's called the frontostriatal pathway and, as you would expect, it's in the prefrontal cortex. Quoting from Dr. Chavez the researcher from Dartmouth on this one, "It connects the medial prefrontal cortex, which deals with self-knowledge, to the ventral striatum, which deals with feelings of motivation and reward." This is a very specific study just in the area of self-esteem and what we're having children experience in these lessons.
This study goes on to talk about a strong pathway that is developed over time, as opposed to what is called traffic on the pathway and could be characterized as incidents or events. Events can make you feel good and important in the moment, however, if you have an overall feeling of self-worth; that path is going to be consistently strong. Even more important is the ability to bounce back, when the event wasn't a positive one and the moment brought pain rather than joy, or feelings of self-esteem.

LESSON FIVE

SING:

Facilitator and children sit on floor in a circle. All sing, "There's Just One Little Nose Like Mine." Sing with music. Facilitator makes an individual comment to each child. For example, "Mario, I like the colors in your shirt. Jarrell, I see you brought your smile today. Mary, are you ready for class?" This sets a positive, caring beginning for the children. All sing "There's Just One Little Nose Like Mine." Sing with music.

FREEZE:

Facilitator says, "When I call your name, run into your own space, and do a freeze. You can freeze any way you want. You can freeze down on the floor. You can freeze with one leg in the air. You can freeze with one hand on your head. You can freeze any way you want. Hold your freeze until all of the children are in a freeze." Facilitator begins immediately calling out their names. After the last child is in a freeze, Facilitator says, "Thank you."

STRETCHING:

Children sit on floor in a straddle position (legs opened). Facilitator asks children to, slowly touch their head to the floor (between child's legs). Then sit up straight. Children do this four times. Children sit facing a partner. If necessary, Facilitator chooses the partners, so that no child feels threatened. Facilitator says, "Hold on to your partner's hands." Children respond. Facilitator asks children, "Sit in straddle position, legs apart." Children respond. Facilitator explains that one of the partners will slowly touch his/her head on the floor, then sit up straight while holding each other's hands. Then the other partner will have a turn. Facilitator asks each couple, "Who will be the first to touch your head to the floor?" Then Facilitator will clap his/her hands every time a child is to touch his/her head to the floor, chanting, "Touching, touching" each time he/she claps. The purpose of this is to provide a non-threatening opportunity for children to physically relate to each other. It also stretches leg muscles. (Some children may not be able to touch their heads to the floor, but they try.) Do this slowly four times.

RUNS: Using Direction (Music, Minute Waltz by Chopin)

Facilitator says, "You are going to run forward today. Go and stand with your back to the wall." Children respond. Facilitator puts on music, and stands with his/her back to the opposite wall. Children run forward. Facilitator asks class to run backward. Children respond. Facilitator asks children, "Run sideways." Children respond. Facilitator asks children to run "other" sideways (actually children are running sideways to right, and then sideways to left).

ARM PATTERNS:

SHOW:
The Facilitator says, "Choose an arm freeze." Children respond. Facilitator stands with her/his back to the opposite wall.

DISCUSS:
Facilitator asks, "What kind of arm freeze would you like to do? Show me." Children respond.

APPLY:
Facilitator stands with her/his back to the opposite wall and claps the gallop rhythm (clap <u>clap</u>, clap <u>clap</u>), while she/he chants or sings. "Galloping forward, galloping forward." Children respond.
Note: Facilitator may need to remind children, "Keep your arm freeze while you are galloping forward."
Facilitator divides group in half. Before each half of the class has a turn to gallop, they choose a different arm freeze.
When both halves of the class have had a turn to gallop forward, all sit in circle. Facilitator says, "Children, now you get to gallop sideways." As the children respond, the Facilitator gives encouragement. For example, the Facilitator might say, "You are working on galloping sideways!" Children sit on their seats and open legs into a straddle, and slowly touches their heads on floor between legs (to stretch leg muscles). Do four times.

CONNECTEDNESS:
"Can your body go fast or slow whenever you want it to?" asks the Facilitator. Children verbally respond. Then she/he asks, "How do you feel about that?" Children verbally respond.

GALLOP: (Using direction)

Facilitator asks children to stand with their backs to the wall. When children comply, Facilitator says, "Children, choose an arm freeze." Facilitator stands with his/her back to the other wall and says, "Gallop forward to me." Facilitator claps rhythm for gallop (clap clap, clap clap). Chanting or singing, "Galloping forward, galloping forward." Facilitator may need to remind children to "Keep your arm freeze while you are galloping forward." Children sit on floor. Facilitator divides group in half. Before each half of the class has a turn to gallop, they choose a different arm freeze. When both halves of the class have had a turn to gallop forward, all sit in a circle. Facilitator says, "Children, now you get to gallop sideways!" Facilitator asks half of the group of children to gallop sideways. As the children respond, Facilitator gives encouragement. For example, the Facilitator might say, "You are working on galloping sideways!" Children sit on their seats, open legs into straddle and slowly touch heads on floor between legs (to stretch leg muscles). Do four times.

EMOTIONAL FEELING – MAD:

Facilitator asks, "Does everyone have feelings? Does your mom have feelings? Does your dad have feelings? Does your sister have feelings? Does your brother have feelings? Do you have feelings? Do I have feelings?" After each question, the Facilitator waits for child to verbally respond. Facilitator says, "Today, we are going to talk about mad feelings." Facilitator says, "Sometimes we feel happy, sometimes we feel sad, and sometimes we feel scared. Sometimes we feel _____" (mad). See if children will supply the word "mad" or "angry." The Facilitator says, "Today we are going to talk about a mad feeling."

SHOW:

The Facilitator shows of picture of someone mad.

DISCUSS:

The Facilitator asks the class, "What is this child feeling?" Children respond.

DISCUSS:

The Facilitator asks the class, "Why do you think this person is feeling mad?" Children verbally respond.

DISCUSS:

The Facilitator asks each child, "What makes you mad?" As each child responds, the Facilitator encourages. For example, the Facilitator might say, "You were mad!" or "That made you mad," or a nod of his/her head.

APPLY:

The Facilitator asks the children to, "Find a space, and do a freeze that tells me you are mad!" Facilitator endorses, "Lemah has a mad freeze. Andrew's freeze is mad." If a child's freeze does not look mad, have the children sit on the floor, and the Facilitator says, "Children, when we feel mad, do our faces look like this?" (Facilitator smiles). Children verbally respond. The Facilitator says, "Children, show me what your face looks like when you are mad." Children respond. Then Facilitator asks children, "Go and do a mad freeze." Facilitator endorses. For example, "Jarrell, your face looks mad. Your hands look mad." Children sit in a circle on the floor.

COPING SKILL:

The Facilitator says, "Is it okay to hit people when we are mad? No, it is not okay to hit people. So, what can we do when we feel mad?" Children verbally respond. As children respond, the Facilitator corrects any inappropriate suggestions. The Facilitator says, "When you feel mad, you can say, 'I'm mad!' "The Facilitator has each child practice the coping skill. For example, the Facilitator would remind Andrew what he said made him mad: "Jarrell takes the truck away." The Facilitator would say, "Andrew, when Jarrell takes the truck away from you, tell me what you will say." Facilitator has Andrew stand up and say with angry face and arms, "I'm mad." Facilitator endorses, "You did it!" Facilitator says, "There are two more things you need to do, and that is to say, 'Give it back. I'll give you a turn when I'm through.' " Facilitator has Andrew practice all three coping skills. Facilitator endorses him. Facilitator uses this procedure to have each child practice the three coping skills. Say, "I'm mad. Give it back. I'll give you a turn when I'm through." Children sit on floor in a circle. The importance of being kind is important for our world to be a kinder, caring place.

LEG LIFTS: (Music, Waltz of the Flowers by Tchaikovsky)

Facilitator says, "Let's give our legs a turn today. Lie down on your backs, please." Children respond. Facilitator claps his/her hands and chants, "<u>Lift</u> one leg; <u>lift</u> the other leg." (Clap hands on underlined word.) Do four times on each leg. Facilitator endorses. Facilitator asks children, "Roll over on your tummies." Children respond. Facilitator says, "You are going to be lifting your legs to the back." Facilitator begins clapping and chanting, "<u>Lift</u> one leg, <u>lift</u> the other leg. You are lifting your leg to the back." Do 3 times on each leg. Children sit in a circle. Facilitator says, "I will put on the music and you can find your own way to do leg lift patterns." Children respond. Facilitator describes what he/she sees. Children sit in circle. Facilitator asks, "How did leg lifts feel today, children?" Children verbally respond.

CONNECTEDNESS:

Facilitator asks, "What would happen if we did not have legs?" If no response, Facilitator might ask, "Could you run?" To get them started thinking, Facilitator asks, "What else would happen if you had no legs?" Children verbally respond. Facilitator asks, "Children, are you happy we have legs?" Children verbally respond.

TURNS:

Facilitator says, "Today, you are going to find some ways to turn. Go stand in your own space and find a way to turn." Children respond. Facilitator describes what he/she sees. For example: "I see turning on two feet. I see jumping and turning," etc. Do for seven or eight seconds. Facilitator and children sit in circle on floor. Facilitator says, "Do you like turning, children?" Children verbally respond.

IMPROVISE: (Music, Opus 39 Waltz in A-Flat by Brahms)

Children sit in circle on floor with Facilitator. Facilitator says, "I hope you like this music I brought today. Each of you find your own way to dance?" As Facilitator puts on music, she/he says, "Find your own space and dance to the music. There goes Jarrell; there goes Andrew," etc. When children have returned to circle, Facilitator asks each child, "How did it feel to dance to the music today?"

CLOSURE:

Facilitator endorses group. For example, "Children, when you were working on a mad feeling today, you worked hard and you stayed with it. I'm impressed." Facilitator endorses self. For example, "I feel good about myself because I worked hard to prepare this lesson to get it just right."

SING:

Facilitator and children sing, "I'm My Friend." Sing with music.

LESSON SIX

By the end of this lesson, the children will be able to do the following:

1. Sing both self-worth songs with familiarity.

2. Upon command, find their own way to freeze.

3. Walk and jump forward, backward and sideways.
   a. Respond to a connectedness question.

4. Arm patterns
   a. Do their own arm patterns in the forward direction, to the side.
   b. Do Facilitator's arm pattern with concepts of slow and fast.
   c. Respond to connectedness questions.

5. Identify the emotional feeling the child in a picture is feeling and respond to questions.
   a. Apply mad feeling in a freeze.
   b. Do coping skills with mad feeling.

6. Find new ways to turn.
   a. Answer connectedness questions.

7. Identify body parts.

8. Lift leg forward, backward and to the side.
   a. Share a leg pattern.

9. Dance to the music in their own way.

10. Hear themselves individually endorsed and the Facilitator endorse him/herself.

PURPOSES FOR LESSON SIX

1. Sing more of self-worth songs from memory.

Brain Connections: In one study-and of course more need to be done- it was found that: "The patients who listened to music had less anxiety and lower cortisol than people who took drugs." (Levitine, Internet). There is also evidence that the brain produces less cortisol- meaning less stress-when music is evident in their lives. The guitar I mentioned earlier was very helpful for that son of mine.

2. In goals 2, 3, 4a, 4b, 6 and 8a.
Children are adding new ways to move to their movement 'vocabulary.' They are going deeper into their own creativity, discovering their possibilities.

Brain Connections: (How does movement affect the brain?) For a young child, almost all of the activities, the things they do, and the movements they make, come from emotion. It feels good to do something, so they do it. It feels bad, they don't do it. The brain really doesn't start making decisions (executive functioning) in the prefrontal cortex until it is more developed. That development starts around the age of six or so and doesn't complete its development until somewhere near the age of 25. However, the emotional systems of the prefrontal cortex, as well as the limbic system are clearly working at an early age.

4c. Connect children to themselves and to the world in which they live.

Brain Connections: The preschool ages are the years when children are feeling more than thinking, so understanding their feelings and allowing them to address those feelings in their world, is a very big deal. Preschool is a perfect place with plenty of interaction with others, to try out what they feel and have what works well, be reinforced. One summer I was asked to teach a class for parents of incoming kindergartners who hadn't attended preschool. The school had clearly identified the struggles for those who hadn't attended.

5. Since children with needs have been given the message "don't feel," they need countless experiences with identifying their own and others' feelings and applying them. For children, identifying feelings and applying them, precedes controlling or channeling their feelings.

Brain Connections: Again, most of the brain work at the ages of preschool children involve feelings. Many children come from environments where feelings aren't talked about or are ignored. Do any of you remember when you were told, "Oh, you fell down. It really doesn't hurt"? I do. And it did hurt! So for someone to tell you it's okay to feel scared or angry or hurt is unusual. They may also be telling you it's okay to feel happy and to enjoy the dance, the jumping, or the play. Feelings are okay to have and express. A brain appreciates it.

6. Finding new ways to do things, or exploring (second stage of the creative process), helps children learn to trust themselves. It takes courage to explore or find new ways to do things. Self-trust and self-confidence are interdependent.

Brain Connections: A child's brain is pruning neurons that are not used. The more neurons that are activated, fired, and wired together, the more skills a child has. Explore and learn.

7. Helps all children to become aware, and comfortable with their bodies.

9. Improvising gives more courage to trust themselves.

10. Hearing their own efforts appreciated, and hearing an adult appreciate his/her own efforts, stimulates a child to risk making an effort to get the courage to try. It empowers every child.

Brain Connections: We've talked about a child's body, improvising, and adult appreciation before. Each of these activities affects different parts of the brain and each activates both neurons and memories, positive memories, which become hugely important in the life of both the child and the adult he/she is to become.

LESSON SIX

If Facilitator has not, prior to this class, had a one-on-one experience with each child, have it now. One-on-one experience means a positive interaction between Facilitator and child. For example, Facilitator might say, "Naquita, I saw you help Mary pick up the blocks this morning. How did you feel when you helped her?" Facilitator and children sit in circle on floor.

SONG:
All sing, "There's Just One Little Nose Like Mine." Sing with music. Facilitator says, "We will do today like we did last class. As I call your name, run into your own space and do a special freeze. Keep your freeze until every child in our class is in a freeze." Facilitator immediately begins calling the names. When all are in a freeze, the Facilitator says, "Thank you." Facilitator and children sit in a circle on the floor.

SHOW:
Facilitator asks children to walk forward while she/he sings, "Walking forward, walking forward," as children comply.

DISCUSS:
"Children, could you jump forward?"

APPLY (1):
Children jump forward as the Facilitator claps his/her hands quickly, singing, or chanting, "Jumping forward" repeatedly. Do for six or seven seconds.

DISCUSS:
Facilitator asks, "Children, could you jump backward?" as Facilitator claps and sings or chants, "Jumping backward." Do for six or seven seconds. Facilitator makes an endorsing comment that is also encouraging. For example, "Children, you are listening and doing." Children return to sit in circle.

SHOW:
Facilitator walks sideways, both to the right and to the left.

DISCUSS:
Facilitator asks, "Which direction am I walking?" Children verbally respond.

APPLY: #1
Facilitator asks children to walk sideways, first to one side, then the other, as she/he claps and chants, "Walking sideways."

APPLY: #2
   Facilitator asks children to jump sideways. Facilitator claps and chants, "Jumping sideways" (both to right and then to left). Do for four or five seconds. Facilitator endorses the class. For example, "Jumping sideways is not easy, but you are doing it." Children return to sit in circle.

CONNECTEDNESS:
   The Facilitator asks the children, "What if we could only move forward? What would happen if we could not move backward, could not move sideways – we could only move forward?" NOTE: Predicting will be a new experience for the children. Facilitator will need to wait a moment and patiently repeat the above. If no response, or incorrect response, the Facilitator can ask, "Children, would you like to live in a world where you could not move backward or sideways?" The Facilitator can make the point, "I'm so glad we can move our bodies in any direction. Aren't you?" Children verbally respond.

ARM PATTERNS: (Music, Morning from Peer Gynt Suite by Grieg)
   Facilitator might say, "You've found so many ways to move your arms, haven't you? Today, I want you to find an arm pattern using the forward direction … with your arms in front of you. Forward and in front are the same. Go to your own space." Facilitator immediately puts on music and watches for child who complies. If no child gets it, Facilitator stops music and asks children to, "Put your arms in front of you." When they comply, Facilitator says, "That's it! That's it! Now move your arms right there in front of you." Facilitator gives encouragement. For example, "You're working on it." Facilitator then asks children to put their arms to the side. Children respond. Facilitator asks children to find an arm pattern to the side, and starts the music. Again, Facilitator encourages. Facilitator corrects when necessary. For example, "Mario, move your arms to the side." When child complies, Facilitator says, "You've got it." He/she then asks children to do an arm pattern behind or in back of them. Facilitator repeats the above process. Facilitator stops the music. Then the Facilitator shares an arm pattern with children. It can be an arm pattern in front or to the side, or to the back. Facilitator turns on music and does his/her pattern one time and says, "Do it with me, children," while continuing to do his/her arm pattern. The Facilitator says, "Lemah's doing my pattern. Mary's doing it," etc. Children sit on floor in a circle. Facilitator says, "Children, is there anyone who could do my arm pattern s-l-o-w-l-y?" The children who respond find a place to stand. The Facilitator says, "Do my pattern s-l-o-w-l-y." When the children comply, Facilitator says, "You did it slowly!" Children return and sit in circle. When Facilitator says, "Is there anyone who can do my arm pattern fast?" Children respond. Facilitator says, "You did it!" (Facilitator does not now do pattern. Since Facilitator is testing to see if children understand the tempo concept, he/she does not model it for the children.) Facilitator endorses. For example, "You really did my pattern slow and fast!" Facilitator asks children to sit on the floor.

CONNECTEDNESS:
Facilitator asks children, "What would happen if you had no arms?" Facilitator may need to repeat question, wait for a second, and if there's no response ask, "Could you give someone a hug? How would you eat?" etc. Facilitator asks, "Would you like it if you had no arms?" Children verbally respond.

GALLOP:
Facilitator says, "Go for a gallop. Find your own space." Facilitator claps gallop rhythm pattern: Clap clap; clap clap for five or six seconds. She/he asks, "Which direction are you galloping?" Children verbally respond. Then as children gallop, the Facilitator says, "Gallop backward," and gives encouragement. For example, Facilitator says, "It's not easy to gallop backward!" Facilitator chooses half of the class to gallop while the other half observes. Facilitator endorses each group's effort. Facilitator has children come back to circle and asks, "How do you feel about yourself when you work on something that's hard, like galloping backward?" Children verbally respond.

SHOW:
Facilitator shows picture that goes with this lesson of a child who is mad.

DISCUSS:
Facilitator asks, "How is this child feeling?" Children verbally espond. Facilitator asks, "What do you think might have made this child mad?" Children verbally respond. Facilitator asks each child, "What makes you mad?" Facilitator responds, after each child gives his/her example. Facilitator can say, "That made you mad," or "You were mad," or nods head.

APPLY:
Facilitator asks children to, "Do a freeze that tells me you are mad." Facilitator endorses, "Mary is doing a mad freeze. Mario is doing a mad freeze."

COPING SKILLS:
The Facilitator says, "Last class we worked on what we can do when we feel mad. Do you remember? What can we do when we feel mad?" (We can look mad while saying, "I'm mad!" Facilitator has everyone practice it.) The Facilitator says, "Do we hit people when we're mad? No, we do not hit people, but we can hit stuffed toys. It won't hurt stuffed toys or a bop bag to be hit." The Facilitator takes a stuffed toy and pounds it and kicks it with simulated rage, giving children permission to express their rage. Facilitator says, "When you really feel mad, you can hit a stuffed toy or a bop bag. I want each of you to have a turn." As each child has a turn, the Facilitator endorses. For example, the Facilitator might say, "Naquita is really kicking that bear!" or "Mario, you're not hitting that bear hard enough to be really mad." Mario hits harder and the Facilitator says, "There you go!" When all have had a turn, the bear is put away.

TURNS: (Music, Waltz in C Sharp Minor by Chopin)
Facilitator says, "You are going to turn, children. Find some new ways to turn today. Go find your own space." Facilitator turns on music and describes what he/she sees. For example, "Mario is turning on his back; Andrew's turning on one foot," etc. When children have finished, Facilitator asks children to return and sit in circle.

CONNECTEDNESS:
Facilitator asks children, "What else turns besides people?" When children have responded, the Facilitator says, "Children, did you know our Earth turns? Can we feel the Earth turning? No, we cannot feel the Earth turning, but it does! People can turn; _____ can turn; _____ can turn (naming the examples the children gave). "And the Earth turns!"

BODY AWARENESS:
Facilitator, in a playful mood, covers his/her eyes and says, "When I open my eyes, be touching your shoulders." Children respond. "When I open my eyes, be touching your elbows." Children respond. "When I open my eyes, be touching your 'baby' toes." Children respond. "When I open my eyes, be touching your legs." Children respond. Facilitator makes corrections as needed. Facilitator says, "Children, you are going to do leg lifts today."

LEG LIFTS: (Music, Morning from Peer Gynt Suite by Grieg)
Facilitator asks children to, "Find your own space and lie on your back." Children respond. Facilitator tells children, "You are going to lift each leg forward." Facilitator claps his/her hands once for each leg lift, chanting, "Lift your leg and lift your leg," until children have done leg lifts forward, four times on each leg. Facilitator endorses. Facilitator asks children to get on their hands and knees. Facilitator tells children to lift their legs to the back. Four times on each leg. Facilitator says, "Children, you've lifted your legs forward; you've lifted your legs

to the back. Now, which direction would you lift your legs?" (To the side) Children verbally respond. Facilitator asks children to stand. Facilitator claps his/her hands and chants, "Lift one leg to side, lift other leg to side," until children lift legs four times on each leg. Facilitator endorses. Children and Facilitator sit on floor in a circle. Facilitator says, "You've been lifting legs the way I ask you to. Now, you may have a turn to lift your legs any way you would like to ... in your own leg lift patterns." Facilitator puts on music and all of the children have a turn. Facilitator describes what he/she sees. For example, "Mario is lifting his leg front and then back. Haseem lifts his leg and hops. Naquita's arms are helping while she lifts her leg," etc. After about five or six seconds, Facilitator stops group and the music and says, "Your patterns are coming, aren't they? Let's share. Andrew, do your leg pattern." Facilitator puts on music. Andrew responds. Facilitator says, "All of you try Andrew's leg pattern." Each child who desires may share his/her leg pattern."

IMPROVISATION: (Music, Waltz of the Flowers by Tchaikovsky)

Facilitator says to children, "This is a group who loves to think and to use your ideas." Facilitator chooses half of the class to improvise. Music is quickly turned on, and Facilitator says, "Find a space where there is no other child and dance your own way." As children improvise, the Facilitator endorses. For example, "Lemah's knee is helping her dance. Mary, your pattern matches the music!" Facilitator repeats the above procedure with the other half of the class. Children and Facilitator sit on floor. Facilitator asks, "Children, how did it feel to dance to that music today?" Children verbally respond.

CLOSURE:

Facilitator endorses each child. For example, "Mario, even though you've been coughing today, you still worked hard in class. Jarrell, when I asked you to stop talking, you did!" Facilitator endorses self. For example, "Children, I prepared this lesson so well. I worked hard and I feel good about myself."

SONG:

Facilitator and children sing, "I'm My Friend." Sing with music.

LESSON SEVEN

By the end of this lesson the children will be able to do the following:

1. Sing more of the words of both self-worth songs.

2. Stretch body parts, then answer a feeling question.

3. Run forward, backward and sideways.
   a. Stretch legs.

4. Respond to connectedness question.

5. After identifying something in the room that is straight, do straight leg lifts front, side and back.
   a. Find a different way to do a leg lift and share it with the class.

6. Respond to a connectedness question and find some ways to turn.

7. Identify the emotional feeling of a child in a picture that goes with this lesson. (This is the second time to work with a sad feeling as they did in Lesson Three.) Verbally share an incident when child has felt sad.
   a. Apply sad feeling with a freeze and with walking.

8. Apply coping skills.

9. Gallop, then stretch legs.

10. Respond to the music by doing improvisation (dance their own way).

11. Coping skills with substance abuse such as opioids, other drugs, alcohol and other substances.

PURPOSES FOR LESSON SEVEN

1. Singing self-worth songs uplifts.

Brain Connections: There is a unifying force found in music that is not found in other brain receptors. That unification with others helps a child to identify both with self and those around him/her.

2. Stretching is another way to manipulate their bodies.

Brain Connections: Some children will have difficulty paying attention or staying on task. This may be due to a midline issue. The structure of the brain is such that the right side of the brain controls the left side of the body. Likewise the left side of the brain controls the right side of the body. Movement activity crosses the midline, such as, stretching to one side, then to the other, across the body.

3. Finding different ways to do things like run, leg lifts (5a), and improvisation suggests to a child that he/she can get unstuck from attitudes, behaviors and situations. It gives hope.

Brain Connections: Young children have more neurons than adults so our goal is to keep those neurons firing with activities like running, leg lifts and improvisation. Neurons not fired will be pruned or lost. As a child gets older, neuroplasticity allows for new learning. Learning something new, like playing the piano, is easier for a child because he/she are retaining neurons not building new ones.

4. Connectedness and feeling questions may seem redundant to a Facilitator, but to children, who have been taught to stuff or shut down their feelings, it's like rain to a scorched desert. Children need to better understand their own feelings as well as others' feelings.

Brain Connections: What happens in a child's brain when children learn to shut down their feelings? Feelings are denied or not ever developed. Neurons are pruned. Much is lost. Regaining can be hard but not impossible. Music and movement help.

5. Alternating small muscle activity (such as practicing coping skills) with big muscle activity (such as gallops) is not only restful, but fitting.

Brain Connections: At times feelings can be very powerful, even overwhelming. Practicing muscle activity is like practicing soothing activities for the brain. Practice also helps muscles "remember" what to do. So when those stressful times arrive, the muscles, including the brain and body muscles, know what to do.

6. Children who come from homes with a substance abuse problem need to know what constitutes normal care giving. This motivates a child to seek help when needing care, rather than suffering because he/she perceives neglect as normal.

Brain Connections: A child in a household where substance abuse-including opioids, drugs, or alcohol-is prevalent may not know what normal is. The chaos of an addictive household seems normal if you know nothing else. Preschool is a place where a child can feel safe to trust, feel, and talk. If a child learns to do that, the pathway for self-esteem and emotional balance can work. If the situation is not possible, the child will have a great deal more work to do to develop the neurons lost in those first few years.

If desired, Lesson Seven may be taught in two separate sections, Lesson 7 and Lesson 7a.

Lesson 7 – After Connectedness and Turning, improvise, then close with "I'm My Friend."

Lesson 7a – Sing, "There's Just One Little Nose Like Mine" and begin with Emotional Feeling and complete lesson.

NOTE: When simulated pills are spilled on the floor (Coping Skills), although they are candy, DO NOT allow children to eat them.

LESSON SEVEN

Facilitator endorses children. For example, "I'm glad it's time for this class. Isn't this fun?" Facilitator and children sit in circle on the floor, and sing.

SONG:
"There's Just One Little Nose Like Mine." Sing with music.

STRETCH: (Music, Solveig's Song from Peer Gynt Suite by Grieg)
Facilitator has a rubber band and stretches it. Facilitator asks, "What am I doing with this rubber band, children?" (stretching it) Children verbally respond. Facilitator says, "Children, find your own space." Music is turned on. Facilitator says, "Stretch your fingers … stretch your legs … stretch your feet." Facilitator endorses. Facilitator says, "Rest." Children rest for five seconds, and do it 4 more times. Facilitator asks, "How did stretching feel today, children?" Children respond.

RUNNING: (Music, Minuet Waltz by Chopin)
Facilitator tells children they are going to run backward, sideways and forward. She/he divides the class in half. One half of class stands by wall at one end of room; the other half stands by wall at the other end of room. The Facilitator puts on running music and indicates which group is to run forward. First one group, then the other. When each group has done it three times, the Facilitator stops the music and asks the children to run backward. Facilitator asks the children to face the wall they are standing by (so they are in a position to run backward). Facilitator puts on the music. Facilitator encourages, "You are running backward." When each group has run backward three times, the Facilitator comments, "It's hard to run backward, isn't it?" The children are then asked to run sideways. The music begins, and the Facilitator indicates which group is to go first. Children run sideways both to the right and to the left. When finished, children are asked to sit in a straddle position (legs open) and slowly touch nose to floor between open legs for two times (to stretch legs). Children return to sitting in a circle.

CONNECTEDNESS:
Facilitator asks the children, "Are you glad we can run forward, side and back?" Children verbally respond.

LEG LIFTS: (Music, Minuet in G by Beethoven)

AWARE:
Facilitator asks, "What is something in this room that is straight?" Children respond. Children may say, "The wall is straight," or "The picture is straight," etc. The children are then asked to sit on their seats. Facilitator claps every time he/she says "straight." Facilitator says, "Children, you are going to lift each leg as straight as

the wall. You are going to lift each leg as straight as a _____" (using children's examples of straight). Facilitator claps and says, "Straight as the _____. Straight as the _____," as children lift each leg forward into the air. Do four times on each leg. Facilitator asks children to get on hands and knees. Repeat the same procedure to the back. Facilitator endorses on straight legs. For example, "Children, you are working hard to get your legs so straight!" Facilitator has children stand, and repeat same procedure to the side.

EXPLORE:
Children sit on floor in a circle with Facilitator. Facilitator motivates children to explore (creative process) by asking, "What are some other ways we can do leg lift patterns with straight legs? Who has an idea?" As a child responds, the Facilitator will say, "Let's try it," and each child shares his pattern with the class.

IMPROVISATION:
Facilitator puts on music. For example, Mario does a leg lift while jumping. All the children do Mario's pattern several times as Facilitator encourages. Facilitator asks, "What's a different way to do a leg lift pattern that's straight?" Facilitator repeats above procedure until all who would like to have a turn have done so. Note: If there is no response, or poor response, the Facilitator can say, "How about a leg lift to the side, children? Try it," or, "How about a leg lift with an arm freeze?" Facilitator encourages, "You are doing it!" Children return to sit in circle.

CONNECTEDNESS:
Facilitator says, "Last class we talked about what else turns besides people. Let's talk about that today. What else does turn besides people?" Children verbally respond. IF it is not mentioned, facilitator says, "And out earth turns."

EMOTIONAL FEELING:
Facilitator says, "Let's talk about our feelings, our emotional feelings that we have inside." Facilitator asks children to name some emotional feelings. Children verbally respond.

SHOW:
Facilitator shows sad picture #2.

DISCUSS:
"How is this child feeling?" If children are unable to perceive the child in the picture is sad, Facilitator shows sad picture #1 and repeats question. Make sure each child perceives the child in picture is sad. Facilitator asks each child, "Tell me something that makes you feel sad." Facilitator can respond, when child has finished sharing a sad feeling, by saying, "That is sad," or, "That made you feel sad."

APPLY:

Facilitator asks children to, "Go into your space and do a sad freeze." Facilitator can comment, "Those are sad freezes." If all or most of the children do a sad freeze, the Facilitator then says, "Do a sad walk." Facilitator comments, "Those are sad walks." If there are children whose walks were not sad (they were unable to do the apply step), have all the children sit in a circle. Ask several of the children who were able to do it to repeat it. Facilitator might say, "Haseem, Andrew, and Naquita, you walked so sad. Do it again." They respond. The rest of the children are observing. Facilitator says, "Now the rest of you children do a sad walk." Facilitator may need to remind a child of the example he/she shared about what makes him/her sad, in order to help the child do the apply step. Children sit in circle on floor. Facilitator endorses. Facilitator could say, "The children in this class know about sad feelings!"

COPING SKILLS:

SHOW:

Facilitator says, "When you are feeling sad, you can ask for a hug."

DISCUSS:

Facilitator asks each child, "Who would give you a hug if you asked for one?" Children verbally respond.

APPLY 1:

Facilitator says, "Let's pretend the person you are going to ask for a hug is standing over here (across the room)." "Mary, you said your big sister would give you a hug. Let's pretend I am your big sister standing over here (across the room). I want you to come over here and tell your big sister you need a hug." Have child use this language: "I need a hug. I feel sad." Child responds. Facilitator endorses. This is allowing the child to practice the apply step. Facilitator repeats the procedure with each child, having identified someone who would give a hug. "I feel sad. I need a hug."

SHOW:

Facilitator says, "When you feel sad, you can find a stuffed animal to hug." Facilitator hugs stuffed animal.

DISCUSS:

Facilitator asks each child, "Where can you find a stuffed animal at your house?" This helps the child locate the stuffed animal prior to the need for it, so the child is prepared. If child doesn't have a stuffed animal, a pillow will work.

APPLY 2:
Facilitator has several stuffed animals. Facilitator says, "I am going to pretend this stuffed animal is on Andrew's bed (where Andrew said he could find it). Facilitator puts stuffed animal someplace across the room. Facilitator says, "I am going to put this teddy bear on this pretend shelf where Mario said he could find one." Facilitator continues until each stuffed animal has been placed in a pretend spot where child said he/she could find one. Each child goes one at a time to get his stuffed animal saying, "I feel sad. I need a hug."

GALLOP: (Music, Toreador Song from the Opera Carmen by Bizet)
Facilitator says, "Children, you've been working hard. Go for a gallop and relax!" The Facilitator claps the galloping rhythm (clap, clap, clap, clap) and the children gallop for six or seven seconds. Children sit in a circle on the floor. Facilitator asks all the boys to go for a gallop. Facilitator puts on galloping music and boys gallop. Boys return to sit in circle. Facilitator asks all the girls to gallop. Facilitator puts on music and girls gallop. Girls return and sit in circle. Children sit on their seats and open legs into a straddle. Facilitator asks children to touch their heads to the floor slowly and sit up. "Touch noses on floor slowly. Sit up" (to stretch muscles). Children do this four times. The Facilitator asks, "Did you like galloping to the music?" Children verbally respond.

IMPROVISATION: (Music, Minuet in G by Beethoven)
The Facilitator says, "Today, when you dance to the music, you need to listen carefully to the music because it will give you ideas for your dance. So clean out your ears." Facilitator also "cleans" out his/her ears. Facilitator asks, "Are you ready to listen?" Music is put on. The Facilitator says, "Find your own space and dance your own way to the music." Facilitator encourages, "Lemah is listening to the music," etc. Children and Facilitator sit in a circle on floor.

SUBSTANCE ABUSE INCLUDING OPIOIDS, DRUGS, AND ALCOHOL:
Facilitator holds up picture and says, "Today, children, we are going to talk about drugs. We need to talk about drugs because sometimes children take drugs by mistake. They think drugs are candy. Drugs are not candy. Sometimes people in our families, or people we know, take drugs and cause problems for people in the family and friends. If we put drugs in our bodies, drugs change how our bodies work. Drugs can make us sick if we take them without the doctor's or mom's or dad's help." Facilitator puts down the picture.

COPING SKILLS:
Facilitator puts bottle somewhere on the floor. Open it and let some of the pills (it's candy) spill out. Facilitator says, "Children, never touch anything when you don't know what it is. When you find something, and you don't know what it is, go to a grown-up and say, 'I have something to show you.' Take the grown-up

over to it. Now I want each of you to do it." Facilitator has each child practice the above coping skill. Endorse after each child does it. Facilitator says, "People who drink alcohol or take drugs all the time get stuck to alcohol and drugs, like a piece of paper gets stuck to glue." (Facilitator puts glue on paper and sticks it on another piece of paper while repeating the above sentence.) "When this happens to people, they are sick and need help to stop taking drugs and alcohol. When someone in the family is using alcohol and drugs all the time, that someone may call others bad, bad names, or say things like, 'I hate you. I wish you were dead!' Is it okay for grown-ups to say bad things when they are mad?" Children verbally respond. Facilitator says, "No! Is it okay for grown-ups to say bad, mean things to their families?" Children verbally respond. Facilitator says, "No! It is not okay for grown-ups to say bad, mean things to their families." When someone in the family is using alcohol and drugs all the time, they sometimes hurt children or other grown-ups. Is that okay?" Children verbally respond. Facilitator says, "No! It is not okay to hurt children or other grown-ups."

COPING SKILLS:

Facilitator says, "If you are hurting, you go tell a teacher. You say, 'Teacher, I am hurt,' and you tell the teacher about it." Have each child practice going to you and saying, "Teacher, I am hurt." Teacher endorses each child, "You've got it. When a grown-up in the family is using drugs and alcohol all the time, that person can forget to give children food. Is it okay for a grown-up to forget to give children food?" Children verbally respond. Facilitator says, "No! It is not okay for a grown-up to forget to feed children. Is it okay if a grown-up gives you dinner tonight, but forgets to give you dinner tomorrow night?" Children verbally respond. "Grown-ups in a family should have dinner for young children every night. When you have not been fed, you can tell a grown up." Facilitator asks each child, "If you were hungry and did not have dinner, who would give you dinner?" Each child verbally responds. Facilitator says, "Let's pretend _____ (person whom child identified) is here (Facilitator indicates a spot). Now tell me what you will say. "I'm hungry. I did not get dinner," child responds. Facilitator endorses by saying, "That's right," or, "You've got it." "When a grown-up in a family is using alcohol and drugs all the time, that person forgets about taking care of children. Is it okay for children not to take baths?" Children respond. Facilitator says, "No! Children need baths when they're dirty." "Is it okay if the children wear the same dirty clothes for two or three days?" Children respond. Facilitator says, "Children need to put on clean clothes when the ones they have on are dirty. Children, if grown-ups around you are taking drugs and alcohol all the time, you'll know what to do to get help."

SONG:

Children stand. Facilitator and children sing, "I'm My Friend."

LESSON EIGHT

By the end of this lesson the children will be able to do the following:

1. Sing self-worth songs.

2. Share clapping patterns with each other.

3. Review concept of direction by running front, side and back.

4. Do an arm pattern with only ONE arm at a time, then each child shares one arm pattern with the other children.
   a. Answer connectedness question.

5. Find ways to jump.
   a. Jump applying concept of direction.
   b. Stretch legs.

6. Perceive concept of size.
   a. Apply concept by getting small like small flower and big like big flower.
   b. Find a different way to get little, big.

7. Review leg lift patterns.
   a. Find way to do leg lift pattern.
   b. Some will share their patterns.
   c. Respond to a connectedness question.

8. Listen to Facilitator tell a short story about a child having a bad dream.
   a. Share a scary experience with group.
   b. Apply scared feeling by doing a scared freeze.
   c. Practice coping skills.

9. Dance to the music in their own way (improvisation).
   a. Respond to a feeling question.

10. Verbally endorse self.

PURPOSES FOR LESSON EIGHT

1. When children whose circles of connectedness have been shattered, sing self-worth songs with each other and the Facilitator/teacher, what happens in the brain?

Brain Connections: Singing in a group is uniting. It brings a sense of community. Have you heard that before? I hope so. It's been mentioned and is why these songs are so important. Singing, choral singing, or singing in a group, is uniting. Your brain knows it at a deep level. The two songs help reinforce a child's uniqueness.

2. Opportunities for sharing their own patterns with each other are increasing, to help children break out of any isolation they may have. For children it opens new alternatives. It also adds to their movement vocabulary of both groups. What happens in a child's brain when this occurs?

Brain Connections: Remember the language parts of your brain? They're on the left side and called the Broca and Wernike areas. Lots of parts of our brain light up when sounds, symbols, and new words are introduced. A child's language areas are connecting neurons just by listening and repeating. As language becomes more complex and as vocabulary is developed, more skills are learned. These all help with the very important skills of reading and writing. Practicing oral language now will make reading and writing easier later.

3. Reviewing concepts (direction) and skills (arms, jumping, leg lifts) allows children to improve both in internalizing the concept and improving the skills. Doing something that the child perceives he has done well, builds confidence. What happens in the brain when this occurs?

Brain Connections: The subconscious mind, the remembering brain, cannot differentiate between what is good or bad. It simply records what is experienced, seen or heard. So if a child hears over and over that he/she is stupid or clumsy, the mind will record "I'm stupid." Doing something well changes the thoughts.

4. The concept of size teaches children about the world they live in. Learning the concept of size with objects of nature (in this lesson, beautiful flowers) helps a child relate to his/her inner being, meeting valid dependency needs that all humans have.

Brain Connections: Connecting to what is in a child's world, the world he/she can touch, feel, and see--helps that child know the difference between what is real and what his/her brain stores as memories. In fact each real world connection stores more and better memories in the subconscious brain.

5. All children often feel scared because they know, as children, they are vulnerable. There are some children who feel especially vulnerable. Practicing coping skills helps a child deal with his/her scared feelings.

Brain Connections: Remember the amygdala? It's those almond-shaped pieces in the midbrain that, when activated, can create fear. What resides in the amygdala is often more than fear. It plays a part when our emotions show up the strongest, so fear, anger, sadness, and joy all come from this area. Lisa hit. Althea threw sand. Their anger is coming from the amygdala and the acting out is coming from the emotions triggered by something around them or a memory that has resulted from an event. The more coping skills a child has practiced, the less likely the trigger will activate the negative emotions.

6. Children, hopefully, are becoming more spontaneous in improvisation, indicating an increase in self-trust.

7. Having a child endorse himself/herself teaches the child to identify his/her own strengths. Knowledge of his/her strengths leads to empowerment for all children.

Brain Connections: Improvisation helps the child to be more self-aware and self-trusting. Following up with endorsement reinforces/retains the neurons while activating positive emotions.

LESSON EIGHT

SONG:
Facilitator says, "Let's sing the song that tells you how special you are!" Facilitator and children sing, "There's Just One Little Nose Like Mine." Sing with music.

Facilitator and children sit on floor in circle. Facilitator greets children. For example, the Facilitator might say, "Children, wait until you hear this wonderful music I have for you today! At least I think it's wonderful. You'll hear it in a little while." The Facilitator begins clapping and says, "Let's clap, children." After five or six seconds, Facilitator stops and says, "What's another way to clap, _____?" (choose a child). The Facilitator and children clap the child's pattern as Facilitator sings, "We're clapping on our shoulders with Haseem's pattern."

RUN: (Direction) (Music, Flight of Bumble Bee by Rimsky-Korsakov)
Facilitator asks children to stand with their backs to the wall. The Facilitator says, "I'm going to put on the running music." Facilitator asks, "In which direction shall we run, Andrew – front, side or back?" Andrew responds. Facilitator starts music and the children run in that direction. They do this until children have done all three directions – front, side and back. Facilitator encourages, "Children, you are learning direction, aren't you?"

ARM PATTERN: (Music, Waltz Opus 39 by Brahms)
Facilitator says, "Today, I want you to put one arm behind you and keep it there! Now with your other arm, do an arm pattern." The music is put on immediately and the Facilitator says, "Move into your own space and do your one-arm pattern." Do this until music stops. Then have the children change arms and put the other arm behind. The Facilitator selects a child to share his/her one-arm pattern. Facilitator starts the music. All of the children do that child's pattern. Continue until each child who desires has had a turn to share a one-arm pattern. Facilitator endorses. Children return to sit in circle on the floor.

CONNECTEDNESS:
Facilitator asks, "What would happen if you had only one arm?" If no response, Facilitator says, "If you had only one arm, would it be easy to ride a bike?" (NO) Children verbally respond. Facilitator says, "If you had only one arm, would it be easy to build with blocks?" (NO) Children verbally respond.

JUMPS:
Facilitator claps his/her hands, and says, "Find your own space, children, and go for a jump." While clapping, Facilitator describes what he/she sees. After six or seven seconds, children stop. Facilitator says, "Jump backward." Children respond. Facilitator claps rhythm, and says, "Jump forward." Children respond. After four

seconds, the children are asked to, "Jump sideways." Children respond. Then after four seconds, "Jump the other sideways." Facilitator endorses. For example, "You can jump forward, you can jump sideways and you can jump backward." Children are asked to sit on floor in straddle position (legs open). Children are asked to slowly touch foreheads on ground between legs, then sit up tall. Do four times. This is to stretch and relax the body.

SIZE: (Music, Prelude in C by Bach)

Use big flower and very small flower. Both flowers, big and small, should be the same kind of flower. Do not use silk or any other artificial flowers. Fresh, real flowers must be used. This is a connectedness issue.

SHOW:

Facilitator shows children small flower.

DISCUSS:

The Facilitator asks, "What size is this?" Children verbally respond. If children are incorrect, show both big and little flowers and ask again, "What size is this one?" (indicating little one). Children verbally respond.

APPLY 1:

The Facilitator says, "Find a way to get small as this flower is small." The children respond. Children may need coaching. For example, Facilitator might say, "Mary, look again at how small this flower is." Mary responds. Or, Facilitator might say, "Mario is small." Facilitator says, "All of you get small as this flower." Facilitator might endorse, "You are small." Children return to sit in circle.

SHOW:

Facilitator holds up big flower.

DISCUSS:

Facilitator asks, "What size is this?" Children verbally respond.

APPLY 2:

Facilitator says, "Go to your own space and find a way to get big" (hold up big flower). Facilitator coaches if needed. When all children get big, Facilitator endorses. Facilitator asks each child, "Did you like getting big and little?" Children respond.

APPLY 3:

The Facilitator says, "Now, I want you to find a different way to get little and a different way to get big, as I hold up each flower." The Facilitator puts on the music and the Facilitator holds up the big flower and says, "Find a different way to get to this size." Children respond and the Facilitator endorses. The Facilitator holds up the small flower and repeats the statement. Facilitator endorses. The children return to the circle.

CONNECTEDNESS:

Facilitator says, "Tell me something in this room that is little." Children respond. Facilitator says, "Tell me something in this room that is big." Facilitator asks, "How did you like finding different ways to get big and different ways to get little?" Children verbally respond.

LEG LIFTS: (Music, Minuet in G by Beethoven)

Facilitator says, "Tell me something that is straight." Children respond. Facilitator says, "We are going to do leg lifts. Find a space where no one else is and lie down on your back." Children respond. Facilitator says, "Lift your legs as straight as _____" (using child's image for straight). For example, Andrew might have said the chair leg is straight. Facilitator would say, "Straight as the chair leg." Do four times. Facilitator says, "Children, you are ready to find your own leg lift patterns." Facilitator turns on music and children respond. Facilitator might encourage while children are responding by saying, "Naquita is lifting her leg as straight as _____," (the child's image for straight). Facilitator can say, "I'm looking for leg lifts as straight as _____." Children respond. Facilitator can say, "There you go!" Any child who does a leg lift pattern that is quite straight should be asked to share it with the group so all can try it. Sharing patterns triggers the sense of self-worth in the child. While doing it, the child is reminded to keep leg straight. For example, Facilitator stops the class and says, "Lemah's leg lift is as straight as _____. Watch." Lemah does it. Music starts. All do Lemah's pattern. Facilitator says, "Now, children, do your own straight leg lift pattern." Children respond. Facilitator endorses.

Facilitator asks children to each choose a partner. Children respond. Facilitator asks children to, "Sit in front of your partner and touch your feet to your partner's feet." Children respond. Facilitator puts on music and says, "Lift one leg as straight as _____ (child's image as stated earlier). Put your leg down and touch your foot to your partner's foot." Repeat on other foot. Do four times. Children sit in circle. Facilitator asks each child, "How did you feel about touching your feet to your partner's feet?"

CONNECTEDNESS:

Facilitator asks, "What else has legs besides people?" Children verbally respond.

EMOTIONAL FEELING: Scared

Facilitator says, "Children, all of us have feelings. Let's name some of the feelings." (Happy, sad, mad, scared – these are the only feelings with which we'll be working in this cycle.) Children respond.

SHOW:

Facilitator tells a story about a child having a bad dream.

DISCUSS:

Facilitator asks, "Children, have you ever had a bad dream?" Children respond. Facilitator asks each child, "Tell me about one bad dream you had." Facilitator responds appropriately after each child finishes. For example, Facilitator says, "That would be scary," or nods head, etc.

APPLY:

Facilitator says, "Children, go stand in your own space and do a freeze that tells me you are scared." Immediately the Facilitator begins identifying children who have it. For example, "Mario has a scared freeze. Haseem looks scared."

COPING SKILL:

Facilitator and children sit in circle and Facilitator asks, "Children, are monsters real?" If children seem hesitant, Facilitator immediately answers question, "No, monsters are not real. But when we dream about them, they seem real, don't they?" Children verbally respond. Facilitator says, "The next time you have a bad dream about monsters and you wake up scared, you say out loud, 'Monster, monster, go away. I am safe, I'm okay.' " Children and Facilitator say it together four times. Facilitator endorses.

IMPROVISATION: (Music, Waltz Opus 39 in A-Flat by Brahms)

Facilitator asks, "Children, have you liked the music I brought today?" Children respond. Facilitator says, "I am going to put on some more right now! And you can dance any way you want to." Facilitator chooses half of the class to have a turn. Children respond. Facilitator gives the other half a turn. As each group has a turn, Facilitator endorses. For example, "Haseem's feet are matching the music," or, "Jarrell is doing a leg lift." When all have finished, the Facilitator asks each child, "Tell me how that felt today."

CLOSURE:

SELF-ENDORSING:

Facilitator asks each child, "Since you've been here today, tell me one thing you've done here in class that you've done well." (NOTE – The children will have a hard time remembering and articulating what they've done during class. You may need to review for them. For example, Facilitator might say, "Remember, we found some ways to clap today; we did arm patterns; we did little and big; we worked with scared feelings and danced to the music. What did you do well today?") Facilitator responds to each by smiling, nodding head, or a pat, etc. The purpose of self-endorsing is to teach the children to complement themselves in order to learn how to identify their own strengths. Facilitator endorses him/herself for the same purpose and to model endorsing.

SONG:

Facilitator and children sing, "I'm My Friend." Sing with music.

LESSON NINE

By the end of this lesson, the children will be able to do the following:

1. Sing almost all the words of both songs from memory if teachers are having children sing them at other times during the day.

2. Identify the following body parts: Shoulders, heels, thumbs, elbows, backs, eyebrows and knees.

3. Do knee bounces while in a circle.

4. Identify size of shells (big and little)
   a. Find different ways to get little and different ways to get big.
   b. Respond to connectedness questions.
   c. Find something in the room that is little and something that is big.

5. Run using direction.
   a. Respond to connectedness questions.

6. Find different ways to turn.
   a. Share a turning pattern for the class to do.
   b. Respond to a connectedness question.

7. Listen to a story.
   a. Identify feeling of child in story.
   b. Child tells about a time he/she got lost (if a child was ever lost).
   c. Apply a scared feeling.
   d. Select pictures of appropriate people to go to for help when lost.
   e. Practice coping skill.

8. Dance in their own way to the music (improvisation).

9. Identify what he/she did well in the class.

PURPOSES FOR LESSON NINE

1-3. Singing in unison and moving in unison help a child relate to others in a group. What happens in the brain when this unity occurs?

Brain Connections: Brain studies are showing that both singing and moving in unison increase cooperation and a sense of collaborative effort. There seems to be a belongingness or unity that develops when these events occur.

4a. Reviewing size concept to learn about the world. Using nature objects to teach the size concept helps the child to connect to nature. Becoming aware of his/her inner understanding can meet valid dependency needs and increase children's feelings of security.

Brain Connections: More brain studies are showing the impact of nature, the natural environment, has on the brain. Taking a walk in a forest or on a beach reduces stress and the brain's multitasking. A natural element is relaxing as it creates a sense of well-being.

4a and 6b. Assist the child to come out of his/her aloneness.

Brain Connections: Aloneness in adults leads to all kinds of mental health issues. Often the genesis of that aloneness is in the childhood experience. Having a mom who deeply cares about you, who isn't necessarily perfect, but who genuinely cares about you and what you are, makes that connection. Without having a mom like that, a Facilitator/teacher may help bridge the gap.

4c. Relate size to objects other than shells (broadening application of knowledge). What happens in the brain?

Brain Connections: Brain connections are built through experiences. The more experiences the child has with shape, sizes, color, textures, emotions and more, the more neural connections, memories, and knowledge the child has to work with.

6. Running allows child to use big muscles after using small muscles. This also repeats the concept of direction. The first law of learning is repetition.

Brain Connections: Brain development is about repetition and practice. Hebbs Law says: what fires together, wires together in the brain. Keeping the neurons firing makes for learning.

6a. Child discovers new ways to do the skill of turning.

Brain Connections: These muscle movements and turning activities are connected in the brain's cerebellum as well as the frontal lobe. The frontal lobe is the same place we find the ability for making judgments, feeling remorse, and making moral decisions. Doing movements for children or exercising for adults helps in the decision making development of our brains.

7. For the child to share his/her patterns is to externalize, and for a moment, step out of his aloneness. For each child it affirms his/her creativity.

Brain Connections: Internally there are patterns as well. Many of these patterns show up as positive or negative emotions. Making events positive rather than negative helps a child develop brain patterns that are healthy with a desire to repeat the event.

7a, 7b, 7c. It is scary to begin feeling his/her feelings when a child has been taught to ignore feelings. All pre-school children must learn to identify feelings. To see, hear and apply feelings helps an at-risk child feel his/her feelings.

Brain Connections: Studies are showing that those children deprived of caring interactions don't develop as many brain connections as other children. At-risk children are often told that they don't feel a certain way or it's stupid to feel this or that way. Even more often, the modeling for them is of not feeling. By using opioids, alcohol or other substances adults can avoid feeling anything. Children quickly learn it's not okay to feel. These activities are designed for the child to learn that feeling is okay and it is safe to do so.

7d and 7e. Children may be told what to do in situations, but they are seldom, if ever, given opportunity to practice doing it. Practicing the coping skill helps the child to call it forth when needed.

Brain Connections: Wording is important. We as adults or as a child we are used to others telling us what we think, how we should do things, what's right, and especially how we feel. Our brain gets very used to this outside direction. We hear things like, "That didn't hurt," or worse, "I'll show you something that really hurts." In the activities in this curriculum, we are asking children to discover their inside direction. Infancy and preschool are the years in which we often are conditioned by the adults around us to listen to them. In the process, children will lose the ability to listen to themselves, to their own inner urging and their own creativity.

8. As a child's self-trust increases, the hope for openness becomes a possibility. Every child is growing in self-expression. The child casts a vote for himself/herself. Now what happens in the brain when a child does that?

 **Brain Connections:** Possibilities are what we are creating, lots of possibilities. The music, movement, and opportunities for feeling and self-expression are supportive of all children, and it's specifically important for children coming from families of any sort of addiction or other stressful situations.

LESSON NINE

SONG:
Facilitator and children sit in a circle on the floor. Facilitator says, "Children, is there anyone in the whole world who looks just exactly like you? No!" All sing, "There's Just One Little Nose Like Mine." Sing with music.

BODY AWARENESS:
Facilitator says, "Children, isn't this fun?" Facilitator covers his/her eyes and says playfully, "Touch your shoulders." Facilitator uncovers eyes and endorses (and corrects if needed). Repeat procedure with heels, thumbs, elbows, backs, eyebrows and knees.

Facilitator and children make a circle holding hands; both of each child's feet are together. All bounce their knees. Facilitator chants, "We are bouncing, bouncing our knees!" Do for 15 seconds. Facilitator asks children to stretch their hands and "touch" the ceiling. Children sit on floor in a circle with Facilitator. Children are asked again to stretch their hands as high as the ceiling. Children respond.

SIZE:

SHOW:
Facilitator shows children a beautifully wrapped small box and asks, "What do you think is in this box?" Children verbally respond. The Facilitator says, "Could it be an alligator?" Children verbally respond. Facilitator asks, "Could it be a lamp?" Children verbally respond. Facilitator asks, "Could it be a coat?" Children verbally respond. Facilitator says, "Let's see what it is." Facilitator removes top and lets children look. Then Facilitator lays the shells on the floor.

DISCUSS:
Facilitator asks, "What colors are in these shells?" Children verbally respond. Facilitator asks, "Do you think these shells are beautiful?" Children respond. Facilitator repeats with the other shell. Facilitator puts on music and says, holding up little shell, "Find a space where no one else is, and get this size, children." Children verbally respond.

APPLY #1: (Music, Waltz in A-Flat, Opus 39 by Brahms)
Facilitator puts on the music and says, "Get this size, children (small). If a child does not get small, Facilitator can say, "Mary, can you get small, like this shell is small?" When Mary responds, Facilitator endorses. Repeat the procedure with the big shell. Facilitator stops the music and all of the children sit on the floor in circle.

APPLY #2:
Facilitator says, "Now, children, when I hold up this little shell, find a different way to get little. And, when I hold up this big shell, find a different way to get big. Are you ready? Find your own space." Children respond as Facilitator turns on music.
Have children find two different ways to get big and little. Children respond. Facilitator endorses. Facilitator asks children to sit in a circle.

CONNECTEDNESS:
Facilitator says, "Do you like these beautiful colors?" Children verbally respond. The Facilitator asks "Are you happy to live in a world where there are many sizes?" Children verbally respond. Facilitator says, "So am I!"

SHOW:
Facilitator says, "Show me something in this room that is little.

DISCUSS:
Facilitator asks, "Where in this room is something little?" Children respond. If a child points and says, "That," the Facilitator can say, "Go touch something little."

APPLY:
Facilitator asks children, "Get little like the _____ and _____ and the _____ are little," (naming each item children identified).

DISCUSS:
Facilitator asks, "Where is something in this room that is big?" Children verbally respond.

APPLY:
Facilitator asks the children, "Get big like the _____ and _____ and _____ are big," (naming each item the children identified). Facilitator asks children, "How did you feel about doing little and big today?" Children verbally respond.

ARMS: (Music, Morning from Peer Gynt Suite by Grieg)
Children sit in circle on the floor. Facilitator says, "Since we've been having this class, you have been finding so many different ways to do things! You must like finding different ways to do things. Is that true?" Children verbally respond. Facilitator says, "Move into your own space. Find some different ways to move your arms – to let your arms dance." Facilitator immediately turns on music and chooses four children. As children respond, Facilitator encourages by suggesting, "Arms could go very low or arms could go very high." Facilitator repeats procedure until all have had a turn. Children return and sit in circle on the floor. Facilitator asks

each child, "Did you find a different way to move your arms today?"

DIRECTION: (Music, Minuet Waltz by Chopin)
Facilitator has half the children in the class stand at one end of the room. The other half remain seated in circle on the floor. Facilitator puts on music and asks children who are standing, "Run forward to this end of the room." Facilitator points to the end of the room where the children are to run. Children respond. Facilitator asks the children to run forward again (back to where they began running). The children respond. Facilitator asks, "What direction were you running?" (forward) Children verbally respond.

Facilitator asks children to, "Find a special way to hold your arms while you run—an arm freeze." As children respond, the Facilitator says, "While you hold onto your arm freeze, face this way." Facilitator indicates the direction all of the children are to face to run sideways. The music begins and the Facilitator comments, "You're running sideways, keep your arm freeze." The Facilitator says, "Hold on to your arm freeze and run the other sideways." Children respond. Repeat two times. Music is stopped. Facilitator tells children, "You are going to run backward. Hold on to your arm freeze." Music begins and children respond. Do three times. Facilitator says, "Now you children who have waited so well may have a turn." Facilitator repeats forward, side, and back runs with this group. Children sit in circle on the floor. Facilitator endorses, such as, "You know your directions."

CONNECTEDNESS:
Facilitator asks, "What if you could only move sideways? What if you could not move forward, and you could not move back?" Give children time to ponder this. Then Facilitator asks, "Would you like that?" Children verbally respond. Facilitator asks, "Children, are you glad you can move forward, backward, and sideways?" Children verbally respond. Facilitator says, "I'm glad, too."

TURNS: (Music, Tales of Vienna Woods, by Strauss)
Facilitator asks all the children to, "Find a space where no one else is and find a way to turn." Music begins. As soon as one child begins turning, Facilitator describes what he/she sees. For example, "Haseem is lying on his side and turning. Mary is turning (rolling) over and over," etc. When all have been turning for four or five seconds, Facilitator stops music and says, "Come and sit down, children." Children respond. Facilitator initiates exploring (second stage of creative process) by describing what he/she saw. For example, "You were turning on, one foot; you were turning on your side; you were turning over and over. How else can you turn?" If no response, Facilitator asks, "What part of yourself could you turn on besides your feet?" As each child responds, Facilitator says, "Show me." Child responds. If a child does an unusual turn, Facilitator says, "Children, do Naquita's turning pattern with her." Remember, sharing patterns triggers the sense of confidence in the child.

Children respond. Repeat process until every child who desires has a turn to share. Children return and sit in circle on floor. Facilitator asks, "Are there many ways to turn?" Yes, there are so many ways to turn, and you found some of them today!"

CONNECTEDNESS:
Facilitator asks, "Children, what else turns besides people?" Children respond. (Our Earth, wheels, merry-go-rounds, CDs, microwave plates, etc.) Facilitator asks, "How did turning feel today?" Children verbally respond.

EMOTIONAL FEELING: Scared (no music)

SHOW:
Facilitator says, "Children, we are going to talk about feelings. I am going to tell you a story. One day a lady was shopping in a big store. While she was buying some things, she saw a boy just about your size walking down the aisle all by himself. He was crying. Now this lady was a grandma, and she knew this little boy was lost. He had come to this big store with his family, but had gotten lost. He couldn't find his family. The grandma lady helped him find his family."

DISCUSS:
Facilitator says, "When that little boy couldn't find his family, do you think he felt scared?" Children verbally respond. Facilitator says, "Yes, he felt scared."

DISCUSS:
Facilitator asks each child, "Have you ever been lost?" If answer is affirmative, Facilitator says, "Tell me about it."

DISCUSS:
When each child has had a turn, Facilitator asks, "How did you feel when you were lost?" Children often confuse sad or mad with scared. Help children identify accurate feeling of scared. For example, if child said, "I felt sad," Facilitator can say, "That's not a sad feeling. That's a scared feeling. When we are alone and lost, we feel scared."

APPLY:
Facilitator says, "Children, find your own space and do a walk that tells me you are scared." To help the children begin, the Facilitator repeats, "Do a walk that tells me you are scared." As soon as even one child begins, the Facilitator says, "There goes a scared walk. Naquita, your walk tells me you are scared." When all have done a walk with a scared feeling for four or five seconds, the children return and sit in a circle on the floor. If children capture scared feelings, they will walk with their bodies pulled into themselves, their hands to their faces, or in a protective position.

COPING SKILL:
The Facilitator says, "Children, if you should get lost and can't find the person who is taking care of you, this is what you do: You look for a grandma lady and tell her you are lost, or you look for a mommy with small children." Facilitator repeats. "You look for a grandma lady or a mother with small children and tell that lady you are lost."

SHOW:
The Facilitator shows a picture (#1) of a grandma.

DISCUSS:
Facilitator asks, "Is this a grandma lady?" (Yes) children verbally respond.

SHOW:
Facilitator shows picture (#2).

DISCUSS:
"Is this a grandma lady?" (No) Children verbally respond

SHOW:
Facilitator shows a picture (#3).

DISCUSS:
"Is this a grandma lady?" (Yes) Children verbally respond.

SHOW:
Facilitator shows a picture (#4).

DISCUSS:
"Is this a grandma lady?" (Yes) Children verbally respond.

SHOW:
Facilitator shows a picture (#5).

DISCUSS:
Facilitator asks, "Is this a lady with small children?" (No) Children verbally respond.

SHOW:
Facilitator shows picture (#6).
DISCUSS:
"Is this a lady with small children?" (Yes) Children verbally respond. Facilitator endorses.

SHOW:
Facilitator shows picture (#7).

DISCUSS:
Facilitator asks, "Is this a lady with small children?" (Yes) Children verbally respond. Facilitator endorses.

APPLY:
Facilitator says, "Now I'm going to put 'lady with the small children' and grandma lady' pictures on the wall, and I want you to walk up to one of them and say, "I'm lost. Will you help me?" Have each child choose whether to walk up to grandma lady, or the lady with small children. Then have each child speak loud enough. Facilitator endorses. For example, "You will know just what to do if you get lost."

SHOW:
Facilitator says, "Two other people who will help you are a policeman and a policewoman." Show pictures.

DISCUSS:
Facilitator asks, "Children, who is this?" (Shows picture of policeman) Children verbally respond. Facilitator asks, "Who is this?" (Picture of a policewoman)

APPLY:
Facilitator says, "I'm going to put these pictures of the policemen and policewoman on the wall. I want you to walk up to one of them and ask. "Are you a policeman?" If they say 'Yes,' you say, 'I'm lost." Will you help me?'" Facilitator has each child do it. Facilitator endorses each child, "You'll know just what to do if you get lost."

IMPROVISATION: (Music, Nocturn in E Flat Minor by Chopin)
Facilitator says, "Children, I like the way you are thinking and doing today. I'm going to put on the music, and you may find your own way to dance. Lemah, Haseem, Jarrell, and Mary may have a turn." Facilitator endorses by describing what he/she sees. For example, "Jarrell is dancing down on the floor." Each child has a turn. Facilitator asks each, "How did it feel to dance to the music today?" Children verbally respond. As children dance, Facilitator may need to stimulate ideas by making suggestions. For example, "Children, a leg lift can help you dance. Haseem, let your arms help you dance."

CLOSURE:

Facilitator asks each child, "What did you do well in this class today?" (This is for the purpose of helping a child to become aware of his/her progress and strengths.) Facilitator may have to review the activities then repeat the question. If still no answer, Facilitator might say, "What about _____?" mentioning one thing the child did well. "Do you feel you did _____ well today?"

Facilitator asks, "Children, who is your special friend?" (I'm My Friend)

SONG:

All sing, "I'm My Friend." Sing with music.

LESSON TEN

At the end of this lesson, the children will be able to do the following:

1. Catch the vision of some of the concepts in these two self-worth songs.

2. Listen while Facilitator verbally explores new ways to do freezes.
   a. Upon command, do a freeze. One or two children may share theirs.

3. Run while keeping their arms in a freeze.
   a. Verbally identify the direction they were running.
   b. Run sideways with arms in a freeze.

4. Move their arms slowly, then fast.
   a. Do arm pattern Facilitator shares.
   b. Do their own arm patterns.

5. Respond to questions about flowers, and about size.
   a. Get little when little flower is held up. Get big, when big flower is held up.
   b. Find something on himself/herself that is little, then big.

6. Find different ways to turn.
   a. Respond to connectedness question.
   b. Listen while Facilitator makes a relevant point.

7. Look at a picture and respond to questions.
   a. Child verbally shares an example of a bigger child hurting him/her.
   b. Respond to feeling question.
   c. Apply scared feeling while doing a freeze.
   d. Practice coping skills.

8. Verbally respond to questions that suggest new ideas for improvising.
   a. Improvise.
   b. Child identifies one thing he/she did well in class.

PURPOSES FOR LESSON TEN

1. Catching the vision of some of the concepts in songs can be evidenced by child singing or trying to sing, and being involved.

Brain Connections: In case you're wondering why all this singing is so important, an article in Early Childhood Connections states: "Music engages the brain while stimulating neural pathways associated with such higher forms of intelligence as abstract thinking, empathy, and mathematics." We've already talked about the bonding that goes on in a group when singing is a part of the activities.

2. 2a, 4a, 4b, 6, 8, 8a Exploring new ways to do things (second stage of the creative process) builds flexibility into the rigid little persona of the needy child. A child uses exploration to extend his self-expression and to disclose himself to himself. What happens in the brain when this occurs?

Brain Connections: Carol Dweck has done some groundbreaking studies on mindset. She identifies a fixed and a growth mindset. The rigid persona is often in a fixed mindset, while the child with a growth mindset is exploring and creating, using their talents to find new ways of thinking and doing. A growth mindset can be fostered, and preschool is the place to begin letting a child self-express and explore other possibilities. This also fosters more neural pathways and flexibility in the brain development of the child.

3. 3a, 3b, 4 Gives both at-risk and low-risk children opportunities to practice concepts and skills in their kinesthetic modality.

Brain Connections: You'll notice that these activities have a great deal of movement with little Facilitator-/teacher-directed modeling. There's a good deal of child oriented discovery. There's lots of self-discovery happening. Practice and repetition help development and retention of the neural pathways in the brain.

5. 5a Reviews size concepts through nature objects and great music. Nature and great music help the child relate to his/her sense of self and others and sense of mindfullness.

Brain Connections: Brain studies show that music can have a calming effect and help release dopamine into the system. The jury is still out on whether classical music makes you smarter.

7a, 7b, 7c, 7d Just to be feeling feelings and sharing them, through the safe medium of movement, is relieving and fear-reducing. For the low-risk child this builds confidence that he/she can cope in the situation.

Brain Connections: Many children come with fears and stressors that we as Facilitators/teachers know nothing about. They live with these fears day in and day out so they have come to see the behaviors of those around them as normal. These children are often unconsciously looking for way to stay safe. Asking them about their feelings is sometimes like asking a rock to tell you how it feels. They just can't do it. They have shut down their feeling because so much of it is coming from the amygdala, prior memories and fear. Movement allows them to feel an inner safety.

8a. Child is daring to trust self. Some may be crossing over into self-expression. Improvisation is for self-expression.

8b. Since at-risk children often view themselves as non-persons or objects, to be in a position to again cast a vote for himself/herself is a long way to come toward self-confidence. For the low risk child it reinforces a child's worth. What does that do in the brain?

Brain Connections: The retention and strengthening of neural pathways has been mentioned several times. It's worth noting again. The more practice a child gets in developing his own sense of worthiness, the stronger the neural pathway. At-risk children often hear how "stupid"-or other terms of unworthiness-they are. We can help build neural nets of worth and value by having a child experience that worth again and again.

LESSON TEN

Children and Facilitator are seated in a circle of the floor.

SONG:
Facilitator and children sing, "There's Just One Little Nose Like Mine." Sing along.

SHOW:
Facilitator say, "Today we are going to do freezes."

DISCUSS:
Facilitator says, "Before we do, let's talk about how you could do freezes. When you are doing a freeze, could one leg be in the air?" Children verbally respond. Facilitator asks, "Could you freeze?" Children verbally respond. Facilitator asks, "Are you ready to freeze?" Children verbally respond.

APPLY:
Facilitator says, "When I call your name, run into your own space and do a freeze. You must hold your freeze until every child has had a turn. Okay?" Children verbally respond. Facilitator quickly calls each name. If a child is just standing, the Facilitator encourages. For example, "Mary, let your arm help you in your freeze." Facilitator endorses. When there is an unusually creative freeze, the Facilitator will allow all the children to try it. For example, the Facilitator could say, "Children, look at Eliza's freeze. That looks like fun! Try it, children." Children return and sit in a circle.

RUN: (Music, Flight of the Bumble Bee by Rimsky-Korsakov)
Facilitator says, "Today, when you run, you have to keep your arms in a freeze." Facilitator chooses half of the children, "Find a space where no one else is standing. Now put your arms in a freeze." Facilitator puts on music and children run for nine or ten seconds. Facilitator stops the music and asks "Children, did you keep your arms in a freeze while you were running?" Children verbally respond. Facilitator tells children to run backward. Facilitator says, "Hold your arms in a different freeze while you run backward, children." Children face the wall at one end of the room. Facilitator starts the music, and children respond. Children run backward for nine or ten seconds. Facilitator stops music and asks, "Children, which direction were you running." Children verbally respond. (Backward) Facilitator says, "I saw Andrew's arms in a freeze while he was running backward."

Facilitator has children stand at one end of the room, all facing same direction. Facilitator says, "Children, run sideways with your arms in a freeze." Facilitator starts music and children respond. The children then run sideways the other direction. Facilitator endorses group. Facilitator repeats the same procedure with the other half of the class. Children return and sit. Facilitator asks, "Do you like running backward and sideways?" Children verbally respond.

ARMS: (Music, Morning from Peer Gynt Suite, by Grieg)

Facilitator asks children to move away from each other. Children respond. Facilitator asks children to "Find a way to move your arms s-l-o-w-l-y." (no music) Andrew's arms are s-l-o-w. Lemah's arms are s-l-o-w." When all have responded, the Facilitator says, "Move your arms fast! (no music) Move your arms fast!" Facilitator endorses. Facilitator says, "Children, I have an arm pattern to share with you today." Facilitator puts on the music and does a simple arm pattern. For example, Facilitator takes both hands and describes a rainbow (or arc) moving arms from right to left. Stretch arms straight. Repeat several times. Facilitator says, "Do it with me, children." Facilitator might say, "You did my pattern just right! Now do your own arm patterns!" Children respond. Children sit in circle on the floor.

SIZE:

Big flower, very small flower. Use a different kind of flower than used in Lesson #8. For example, if roses were used in an earlier lesson, use daisies for this lesson.

SHOW:

Facilitator puts a big flower and a little flower on the floor.

DISCUSS:

Facilitator asks, "Children, do you think these flowers are pretty?" Children respond. Facilitator gives his/her opinion. Facilitator asks, "What colors are they?" Children respond. Facilitator allows each child to hold flower for a moment. Children return flowers to Facilitator. Facilitator holds up small one and says, "What size is this?" Children verbally respond. Facilitator repeats procedure with the big one.

APPLY: (Music: Waltz in E-Flat Minor by Chopin)

Facilitator says, "When I call you name, fine your own space and do a freeze this size" and hold up a little flower. Children respond. Facilitator says, "Now do a freeze this size" and holds up a big flower. Facilitator puts on music and says, "Do a different freeze each time." The Facilitator repeats with little flower then with big flower, until children have done each size three time. Facilitator endorses.

TURNS: (Music: Minute Waltz by Chopin)

Facilitator puts on music and says, "Children, find some ways to go for a turn." Children respond, and Facilitator describes what he/she sees. When there is an unusual turning pattern, Facilitator stops group and says, "Jarrell's turning pattern looks fun. Do it, Jarrell." All children do it. Facilitator endorses. Others may want to share their patterns.

CONNECTEDNESS:

Facilitator says, "Children, tell me something at your house that turns." Children respond. Facilitator says, "We've talked about how our Earth that we live on turns. And it's very important that our Earth turns because that turning is what causes night and day." Facilitator concludes with, "Turning is important in our lives."

EMOTIONAL FEELING:

Facilitator says, "We are going to talk about feelings now."

SHOW:

Facilitator shows picture of big child hurting little child.

DISCUSS:

Facilitator asks each child, "Has this happened to you, where an older child is hurting you? Tell me about it." Children respond one at a time. Facilitator asks, "How did that make you feel?" (scared) Child verbally responds

Facilitator asks, "How is this child feeling?" pointing to small child. (scared) Children respond. If child says another feeling, correct the child. For example, "This child is feeling scared."

APPLY:

Facilitator says "Find your own space, children. Do a scared freeze as if a bigger child was hurting you. Children respond. Facilitator coaches, "What do your arms do when a bigger child is hurting you?" Children respond. Facilitator says, "Find a different freeze that tells me you are scared. " Facilitator endorses.

DISCUSS:

Facilitator asks each child, "Has this happened to you, where an older child is trying to hurt you? Tell me about it." Child responds. Facilitator asks, "How did that make you feel?" (scared) Child responds.

APPLY:
Facilitator says, "Take a freeze that tells me you are scared. Think about when the bigger child was hurting, or trying to hurt you." Children respond. Facilitator endorses and/or corrects children. For example, "Jarrell, you look scared." Or Facilitator would correct, "Andrew, what do you do with your arms when someone is trying to hurt you?" Children respond. Children return and sit in circle.

COPING SKILLS:
Referring back to the second discussion step when Haseem said his big brother hurts him, the Facilitator asks, "Haseem, when your big brother starts hitting you, get away from him. Where can you go to get away from him?" Child responds. For example, Haseem may say if he ran outside, he could get away from his big brother. Facilitator says, "Let's practice that, Haseem. Let's pretend this part of the room is outside." Facilitator goes and stands there. "Show us what you will do when your big brother starts hitting you." Haseem runs "outside." Facilitator endorses Haseem. Use the above procedure for each child (which is to review the child's example in the second discuss step and identify for the child where in the room the "get-away place" is and have the child practice). Facilators: do Not rush this. The child getting away is vital. Check back with child to see how this coping skill worked for him/her.

CONNECTEDNESS:
Facilitator says, "Tell me something on you that is little." Children respond. Facilitator says, "Tell me something on you that is big." Children respond. Facilitator might endorse by saying. "Your eyes are really learning to see little things and big things!"

IMPROVISATION: (Music, Waltz in C-Sharp B Minor by Chopin)
Children sit in a circle on the floor. Facilitator says, "When I put on the music and you dance any way you want to, could you dance lifting one leg" (Yes) Children verbally respond. Facilitator asks, "Could you dance down on the floor?" (Yes) Children verbally respond. Facilitator asks, "Could you do a leap?" (Yes) Children verbally respond. "Could you lift one arm high?" (Yes) Children verbally respond. Facilitator starts music and says, "You may dance, children." (If not enough space, select four children to have a turn. Facilitator endorses any pattern that uses a leg lift, a movement on the floor, or a leap, or lifting one arm. For example, Facilitator says, "Andrew's lifting one leg up, Lemah's dancing on the floor," etc.) When all have finished, Facilitator asks, "Children, when you are dancing your own way, is it fun to try new patterns?" Children verbally respond.

CLOSURE:

Facilitator says, "Children, you are really learning, aren't you?" Facilitator asks each child, "Tell me one thing you did well in this class, today." If child says, "I liked _____," confusing like with doing well, the Facilitator can say, "You liked _____. Do you feel you did that well, today?" If child responds positively, the Facilitator can say, "I thought you did too." Some children need real encouragement `

SONG:

Facilitator asks, "Who is your very special friend? (I'm My Friend)" All sing, "I'm My Friend." Sing with music.

LESSON ELEVEN

By the end of this lesson the children will be able to do the following:

1. Sing both self-worth songs.

2. Clap Facilitator's pattern and share one of their own clapping patterns.

3. Gallop to music.
   a. Answer a feeling question.

4. Identify an object in the room that is straight.
   a. Lift straight legs using the direction concepts.
   b. Do their own leg lift patterns to music.
   c. Answer a feeling question.
   d. Answer connectedness questions.

5. Use crystals to review size concept through movement.
   a. Find different ways to get little and big.
   b. Answer connectedness questions.
   c. Use crystal from nature along with desired music to connect child with love and peace.

6. Find their own ways to jump.
   a. Some may share one jumping pattern with the group.
   b. Leg stretches.

7. Verbally review emotional feeling.
   a. From two options, each child will select one and practice coping skills.

8. Endorse himself/herself.

PURPOSE FOR LESSON ELEVEN

1. Some children may be understanding many concepts in these songs.

Brain Connections: Practice brings more understanding and awareness, and as their neurons fire together they wire in these understandings.

2, 4b, 5b, 6, 6a, and 8. In the process of uncovering their creativity and inner beauty, the children are disclosing a sensitive part of themselves. Two wholeness processes are occurring--they are risking (trusting themselves enough to risk), and they are making life--changing discoveries about themselves.

2. Using big muscles to music has exhilarative value.

Brain Connections: Movement allows both creativity and connection for the body and the brain. There are neurons in the body, not just in the brain. Movement allows the connections to be made from brain to heart to stomach.

7 and 4a. A new standard is being set. Not only will the child lift his/her legs, but the child will work on lifting a straight leg. Remember, low parental standards are a risk factor. As a child conquers a skill or concept, new expectations are necessary. The new skill or concept needs to be developmentally appropriate. Helping the child meet new expectations that are sequential and appropriate is Facilitator's job.

Brain Connections: What happens in the brain? New skills bring more neural brain connections. These new ideas keep the neurons from being pruned.

4. Crystals from nature are used with classical music coupled with the child's own movement modality, connecting the child to the wholeness within. The child's self-worth is totally engaged. What happens in the brain?

Brain Connections: There are neurotransmitters (chemicals) that, when released, create total engagement. Those transmitters include: serotonin, dopamine, cortisol and norepinephrine. When a child is completely absorbed, you'll see that absorption in the brain system. You'll also see a whole child for the moment or for that period of time.

5. Children are frightened when they hear adults fighting. Practicing how to handle that situation may lessen their fear, and may help to keep the child safe.

Brain Connections: When others are fighting around you, the amygdala is going to react with fear. This is especially true if there is a history--i.e. you have a memory of fighting going on regularly. If someone gets hurt, either physically or emotionally, the memory is very strong. These memories include a strong emotion and therefore the brain and body react. At first it may be a conscious reaction because a child is in the midst of the fight, but if fighting happens often, a child may react to the memory of a past fight, and can project the previous event into what can happen now. Someone, maybe the child, is going to get hurt. Leaving the room or having the child express their fear, "you are scaring me," may get the attention of the combatants. Or it may not. Another way to deal with a fear is calming the mind. Calming the mind helps the brain go from the amygdala to the prefrontal cortex where decisions can be made and fear can dissipate.

8. Child gets to consider one effort he/she has made during class, and verbally applaud for himself/herself.

LESSON ELEVEN

SONG:
　　Facilitator says, "Let's sing, children." All sing, "There's Just One Little Nose Like Mine." Sing with music.

CLAPPING:
　　Facilitator says, "Let's clap." While Facilitator and children clap, Facilitator says, "I'm going to be the first to share a clapping pattern today, children." Facilitator chants while all are clapping, "We're clapping our hands with (Facilitator's name) a pattern." She/he claps on elbow. Facilitator gives each child who would like to a chance to share a clapping pattern. Facilitator endorses group. For example, "You found lots of different ways to clap, today."

GALLOP: (Music, Toreador Song from Carmen by Bizet)
　　The Facilitator says, "Children, I have some galloping music today. You may gallop any way you would like to." Facilitator has one half of the class find their own space. The music begins, and the children gallop. Facilitator asks, "How did galloping feel today?" Facilitator repeats the same procedure with the other half of the class. Children sit in circle on the floor.

LEG LIFTS: (Music, Fur Elise by Beethoven)
　　Facilitator asks children, "Tell me something in this room that's straight." Facilitator selects one child to respond. Facilitator says to all the children, "Find a space where no one else is, and lie down on your backs." Children respond. Facilitator says, "<u>Lift</u> your leg as straight as _____ (using child's image) and put it down." Children respond. Facilitator says, "<u>Lift</u> other leg forward as straight as _____ (child's image) and put it down. Facilitator claps his/her hands and says, "Straight as _____ (child's image). Straight as _____ (child's image)." Facilitator claps on underlined word. This continues until children have lifted each leg forward three times.

　　Facilitator asks children to, "Tell me something else in this room that is straight." Facilitator selects one child to verbally respond. Facilitator asks the children, "Lift one leg to the back and put it down" Children respond. "Lift the other leg to the back and put it down." Children respond. Facilitator begins clapping his/her hands and saying, "Straight as _____ (child's image), straight as _____ (child's image)." Facilitator continues until children have lifted each leg to the back, three times.

　　Facilitator says, "Children, you've lifted your legs so straight to the front, you've lifted your legs so straight to the back, now, what direction would you lift your legs?" (To the side) Children verbally respond. Facilitator asks the children to stand.

Facilitator asks, "What else in this room is straight?" Facilitator selects one child to answer. Facilitator says to children, "Lift one leg to the side and put it down. Lift the other leg to the side and put it down.

Straight as ____ (child's image), straight as ____ (child's image)." Facilitator continues until children have lifted each leg to the side three times, working on lifting a straight leg. Children return and sit in the circle of the floor. Facilitator says, "Children, I will put on some music and I want you to find your own way to lift your legs straight." Facilitator immediately starts the music, and children respond. Facilitator describes what he/she sees. For example, "I see a leg lifting to the side that is straight. I see two hands on the floor while one leg lifts straight to the back." When Facilitator stops music, he/she says, "Freeze." When all hold freeze, the Facilitator says, "Thank you." Children sit in the circle on the floor. Facilitator asks, "How did it feel to lift your legs straight today?" Children verbally respond.

CONNECTEDNESS:
Facilitator asks, "Are you happy you have legs, children?" Children respond. "What would happen if we had only one leg?" (Pause to allow children to think about it.) Facilitator might ask, "Could we run?" Children verbally respond. "How would we walk?" Children verbally respond. "Could we gallop?" Children verbally respond. "Are you happy you have two legs and not just one?" (Yes) Children verbally respond.

SIZE: (Music, Prelude in C by Bach)
Big and Little

SHOW:
Facilitator puts two crystals (one big, one little) on the floor. Facilitator says, "Children, these are called crystals. They were dug from out of the ground. If you hold up a crystal to the light, you will see colors!" Children take turns holding up a crystal.

DISCUSS:
"What colors do you see?" Children respond. Facilitator says, "Do these crystals sparkle?" Children verbally respond. Facilitator says, "I think these crystals are beautiful! Do you?" Children verbally respond. Facilitator asks, "Which crystal is little?" Children respond. Facilitator asks, "Which crystal is big?" Children verbally respond.

APPLY: Music: Waltz in C-Sharp Minor by Chopin)
Facilitator says, "Show me how big this big crystal is." Facilitator endorses the whole class, "You are big!" if all did it, or Facilitator endorses individuals who did it. Repeat procedure for little size.

Children and Facilitator sit in circle. Facilitator says, "When I hold up each crystal, I want you to find a different way to get big, and a different way to get little. Facilitator turns on the music. Facilitator holds up big crystal and says, "Children, find a different way to get big like this big crystal." Children respond. Facilitator endorses by describing what he/she sees. For example, Facilitator says, "Naquita stretches one leg and both arms in the air to get big. That is a different way to get big, Naquita." Repeat above procedure for little size.

CONNECTEDNESS:

Facilitator asks each child, "Tell me one thing outside that is little." Children verbally respond. Facilitator says, "Tell me one thing outside that is big." (Children may need to look out the window to respond.) Children verbally respond.

JUMP:

Facilitator begins clapping his/her hands and says, "Go for a jump, children." Facilitator chants (as clapping continues), "Jump, jump, jump. We like to jump." Then Facilitator describes what he/she sees. For example, Facilitator might say, "I see jumping with one leg up. I see jumping backward." Children jump about 10-12 seconds. If Facilitator sees an unusual (creative) jump, he/she stops children and says, "Children, Lemah's pattern looks like fun. Do it again, Lemah." Lemah responds. Facilitator says, "Try it children." Facilitator again claps his/her hands to provide a rhythm background for the jumps. Other children may want to share a pattern.

Facilitator asks children to sit on their seats and open their legs (into a straddle). Facilitator asks children to, "Slowly touch your head to the floor between your legs. Then sit up stright." This is to relax and to stretch the leg muscles. Do this s-l-o-w-l-y three times.

EMOTIONAL FEELING: (Scared)

"What feelings have we talked about?" Children verbally respond. (Happy, sad, mad, scared) Facilitator reminds, if the children leave out any of the feelings.

SHOW:

Facilitator says, "We are going to talk about when you hear grown-ups fighting."

DISCUSS:

Facilitator asks each child, "If you are standing right beside these grown-ups when they are fighting, how would you feel?" If no answer, repeat the question. If still no answer, repeat the show step then the Facilitator asks, "If you are in the same room when grown-ups are fighting, how would you feel?" (scared) Children verbally respond. Facilitator asks each child, "What scares you about their fighting?

Are you afraid the two people fighting won't like each other anymore, or are you afraid you might get hurt?" Facilitator has children who are afraid they may get hurt sit on one side of Facilitator, and the other children who are afraid the two grown-ups won't like each other anymore sit on the other side of the Facilitator. (The coping skills for each response is different, so each group will be done separately.) Facilitator says, "If two grown-ups are fighting and you don't feel safe, get out of that room. Go into a different room."

COPING SKILLS:

Facilitator asks the group of children who are afraid they'll get hurt, "If you don't feel safe when grown-ups are fighting, what can you do?" Children verbally respond. (Go into a different room.) Facilitator says, "Let's pretend this is another room (indicating a different part of the room you are in); now here's the fighting." Facilitator says, "Now show me what you will do." Children go into a different 'room.' Facilitator endorses. For example, "You did it, children. You did it!"

Children return and sit in a circle. Facilitator tells the group of children who are afraid the two grown-ups won't like each other anymore, "When two grown-ups are fighting and you are afraid they won't like each other anymore, you can say, "You are scaring me!" Facilitator has each one of the children in that group say loudly two times, "You are scaring me." Facilitator endorses after each child responds. Children sit in circle.

IMPROVISATION: (Music, Tales of the Vienna Wood by Strauss)

Facilitator says, "Children, today when you dance any way you want to, listen to the music. The music will give you ideas for patterns." Facilitator puts on music. As children respond, Facilitator describes new patterns he/she sees. For examples, "Haseem's arm is making circles. Mary's leg is lifting in the back," etc. When music stops, Facilitator says, "Freeze." When all freeze, Facilitator says, "Thank you."

CLOSURE:

Facilitator asks each child, "Did you feel you did well in this class today?" If a child says, "No," Facilitator asks, "What did you not do well?" Child responds. Facilitator asks, "Do you feel you did one thing well, today?" Child responds. Facilitator asks, "What one thing did you do well today?" Facilitator reminds children of movement done today. Facilitator asks that question to each child. Facilitator endorses himself/herself.

SONG:

Facilitator and children sing, "I'm My Friend." Sing with music.

LESSON TWELVE

By the end of this lesson, the children will be able to do the following:

1. Sing songs supplying words Facilitator leaves out.

2. On command, do a freeze with one leg in the air.

3. Respond to a creativity question.

4. Choose a partner, and find his/her own way to do the skills the Facilitator assigns.

5. Improvise to the music.
   a. Respond to feeling questions.
   b. Listen to Facilitator read booklet.
   c. Answer questions.
   d. Practice coping skills.

PURPOSES FOR LESSON TWELVE

1. When singing the songs with the children, the Facilitator can stop singing a word here and there in the song and the children will supply the word. It helps to cue the concept in the child's mind.

Brain Connections: Long-term memories are filtered in the brain through a portion of the limbic system called the hippocampus. Memories are stored in a variety of areas, but they pass through the hippocampus on the way. The more a child practices the songs, hears and says the words, and uses cues to remember the words, the more this helps the hippocampus in its memory work. My own children learned to sing all the nursery rhymes.

2. The children are ready for a new expectation, a new challenge, while doing freezes. One leg must be in the air. How and where, and what they do with the rest of themselves is their choice. How does choice affect the brain?

Brain Connections: In the past we learned to parent and teach authoritatively--sort of the "do as I say" model. However, what we've found is authoritative modeling isn't effective both in developing a sense of wholeness or in brain development. Giving choices allows a child to explore options and for his/her mindset to be in a growth rather than a fixed mode. This is more inner directed that outer responsive.

3. Examining possibilities helps any child to think creatively.

Brain Connections: Creativity requires lots of areas of the brain working together, not just the older belief of the right brain being creative and the left brain hemisphere being logical. The more we allow practice of these kinds of exploratory thinkings and workings, the better for the neural development and the creativity of the brain. Putting a child's art items on the refrigerator with a magnet is a great place to keep some of the creative demonstrations of the budding artists and the creative personalities.

4. Doing a skill one's own way, while another child is doing the same skill in his/her own way, works toward human intimacy in a non-threatening way. When a child's feelings are shut down, the child lacks the capacity for human intimacy (relating with another in warmth and caring). Although human intimacy is longed for, it is often frightening. Encounters with others are necessary, but these encounters initially must be non-threatening. For low-risk children dancing with other children is fun.

Brain Connections: When a child's brain, especially the amygdala, is stressed repeatedly in threatening or what appear to be threatening situations, a child will, for survival, either act out or withdraw (fight or flight). This can become a pattern in all interactions as the child projects the fear into any intimate contact. Practice, and lots of it, in non-threatening situations reduces the fear and anxiety lodged in memory.

5. Improvisation provides another opportunity for self-expression and spontaneity to occur.

Brain Connections: When a child isn't feeling threatened or remembering threatening situations, spontaneity is possible and likely to occur.

5a, b, c, and d. Are designed to protect a child against sexual assault, the most devastating experience a child can have. As a child is endorsed for telling when another child touches his/her private zone, children are more likely to tell if a youth or adult does it. Having each child practice the coping skill, and being sincerely endorsed by the Facilitator, fortifies the child for protection. All children in our society need these skills.

 **Brain Connections:** A sexual encounter in a young child creates a memory, always fear. Often a child will feel they were wrong and the adult was right to do what they did to them. Self-esteem is shattered. They need practice in being safe.

LESSON TWELVE

This is the lesson to teach sexual-assault prevention. Not all adults are at ease with this information. If a Facilitator feels any discomfort teaching this lesson, do not do it, because children soak up attitudes. Ask another Facilitator to teach this portion. If we are to protect our children, a Facilitator who feels comfortable with this material must do this lesson. Asking another Facilitator to teach it demonstrates caring, sincerity, and commitment to children's safety.

SONG:

Facilitator and children sit on floor in a circle. Children and Facilitator sing, "There's Just One Little Nose Like Mine." Facilitator endorses children as a class, about their work in this program. For example, Facilitator could say, "Children, you are learning so well to find your own creativity inside you. That means you are having many ideas about how to do things. You are also finding that deep inside each of you there is lots of beauty. And you are having fun!

FREEZES:

Facilitator says, "When I call your name, run into your own space and do a freeze with one leg in the air." Facilitator selects first a child who will be most likely to understand and do the assignment. Facilitator says, "Jarrell, run into your own space and freeze with one leg in the air." Jarrell responds and Facilitator encourages, "Put one leg in the air, Jarrell," or endorses, "You did it!" Facilitator then quickly calls each child and says, "Find your own way to do a freeze with one leg in the air." When all have responded, the Facilitator says, "Thank you." Children return and sit in the circle. Facilitator asks, "Children, are there lots of ways to do a freeze with one leg in the air?" When all have responded, the Facilitator says, "Thank you." Children return and sit in the circle.

PARTNERS:

Facilitator asks children, "Go and choose a partner." When children have responded, Facilitator says, "Bring your partner and sit in the circle." Children respond. The Facilitator assigns one couple to run with their arms in a freeze. One couple is assigned to gallop. One couple is assigned to do arm patterns. One couple is assigned to do turns. The Facilitator puts on background music, and one couple at a time responds consecutively. Background music, "Dance of the Sugar Plum Fairy" by Tchaikovsky, and should be played all the way to the end. Facilitator endorses children. Facilitator excuses children who have not been cleared to do Sexual Assault Prevention.

SEXUAL ASSAULT PREVENTION:

Facilitator says, "Today we are going to again learn how to help ourselves." Facilitator reads the book Private Zone to the children. Book marked where to interrupt and do coping skills. "You may call your private parts your private zone."

COPING SKILLS #1:

Facilitator asks, "Children, if someone touches your private zone, what do you do?" (They yell and tell.) Have children yell, "Don't touch! That's my private zone!" Have children do it two more times. Facilitator says, "If any one touches your private zone, you yell and tell. Haseem, if anyone touches your private zone, whom would you tell?" Child responds. Facilitator may need to help child identify the person. If child can't think of a person, Facilitator might ask, "Could you tell your mom?" Keep suggesting until child has identified the specific person to tell.

Often a child will suggest the person to tell is another child. The Facilitator can ask, "Is that person a grown-up?" If child says, "No," Facilitator says, "You need to tell a grown-up so you can get help." Have child then select a grown-up to tell.

COPING SKILLS #2:

Facilitator asks each child, "Naquita, if someone shows you their private zone and tells you not to tell or you'll get in trouble, show me what you will do. Let's pretend that _____ (the person Naquita identified as the one she could tell) is over here (indicate the exact spot in the room). Now, Naquita, show me what you will do." Naquita tells. Facilitator endorses, "You would know exactly what to do!" Facilitator goes through this procedure with each child.

COPING SKILLS #3:

Facilitator says, "What if that person shows you their private zone again? Show me what you will do." Have child practice telling again. Facilitator endorses. "That's right! You will tell whenever it happens." Facilitator says, "Children, you are learning to get help when you need it."

SONG:

Children stand. Facilitator says, "Let's sing, "I'm My Friend.'" Sing with music.

LESSON THIRTEEN

By the end of this lesson the children will be able to do the following:

1. Sing both self-awareness songs, supplying the words the Facilitator leaves out such as: "There's just one little _____ like mine. It belongs to _____."

2. Identify objects that are high and low. Then demonstrate their understanding of these concepts through movement (freezes).

3a. The children will review size concept using crystals .

3b. The children will improvise using the size concept as part of improvisation.

4. Answer questions.

5. Hearing the rhythm of their names, the children will match that rhythm by doing freezes.

PURPOSES FOR LESSON THIRTEEN

1. While singing the self-worth' songs with the children, the Facilitator can stop singing phrases here and there. It will help cue the concept in the child's mind.

Brain Connections: Self-worth is very important for a child's brain development. This kind of activity stimulates various parts of the brain at once, as well as creates patterns for the neurons that fire and wire together. Now there is a need to remember the words. Memories come with some sort of emotion, so the limbic system is involved. The language system comes into play when a child needs to articulate something remembered. Children are modeling something positive that they recognize. With all their practice they can now see it in themselves.

4. The children are progressing. They are ready for a new concept, which is high and low. What happens in the brain when new concepts occur?

Brain Connections: Brain development is dependent in early childhood on what's called "serve and return." Like in tennis, you serve the ball and in order to play the game, it's returned. For a child, a new concept needs to be served and they return it for learning or a connection to be made. Serve the new idea and wait for the return. Serve again if necessary. Let the concept connect.

5. The children are asked to do jumps using the concept of high and low.

Brain Connections: For the skill to be learned, it needs to be practiced. The brain needs to fire and wire the neurons of this new skill. A new skill requires practice and then more practice until it becomes habitual. The brain loves to habituate what we do.

6. Stretching relaxes their legs after strenuous use of leg muscles.

7. Using their arms only, the children apply the concept of high and low, learning to think creatively.

Brain Connections: As a child grows, so does his/her brain and its capacity to think. An infant and toddler is all about feeling. The older a child gets, beyond the preschool ages, the more his/her prefrontal cortex comes on line. Thinking and decision making is possible generally around the age of 7 or 8. When a child can combine thinking with feeling, then there is real creativity because you now have both skills.

8. By continuing to learn to think creatively, the children will respond to connectedness questions.

Brain Connections: Connections from their brains and its feeling and thinking to their bodies as well as connection to those around them, creates the patterns of self-awareness and wholeness we are striving for.

9. Rhythm is one of the building blocks for reading. Working with rhythm prepares the child, later on, to read. When using the process for learning concepts (show-discuss-apply), the child is able to learn the complicated process of rhythm.

Brain Connections: Brain studies are showing that a brain seems to synchronize itself with music, a beat--in other words, a rhythm. It isn't that a child is smarter if Mozart is in the background, but a child does connect with the rhythm. In the same vein, a group of children will synchronize their thinking in rhythm to a beat and to each other. Music soothes and makes new concepts like reading, easier. The sense of mindfulness: the beauty within nature and each child is activated with classical music. Our current music is a good rhythmic beat, but it isn't necessarily the soothing rhythm the brain needs for conscious awareness (being in the present moment).

10. This is the first time the children have been asked to use a concept while improvising. During their improvisation, the Facilitator will say, "Keep your dance going, but dance on the low level." After the children respond, the Facilitator will say, "Now dance any way you want to." Then the Facilitator will say, "Keep you dance going, but dance on the high level." Children respond. Facilitator stops the music and says "Freeze." The Facilitator endorses the children, such as, "You are thinking today, children!"

Brain Connections: The brain develops from back to front and from the inside out. What that means is there are three parts of the brain to develop. The reptilian brain is the brain stem and develops in utero. A baby is born with a reptilian brain, and the will to survive. The reptilian brain keeps the heart beating, the lungs working to breathe, hunger, body temperature, etc. Someone asked recently what the difference was between a lizard baby and a human baby. Well, yes, the human baby cries and keeps you up at night. That is a difference. The big difference is that a lizard mommy has a baby lizard and once it can survive, mom moves on and leaves the little lizard on its own. Human moms keep their babies, toddlers, children and teens for years. Their brains are just not developed for a very long time.

The limbic brain, mid- or mammalian brain is next to come on line. That's where the emotional brain exists and it is dependent on internal and external cues. In early childhood, until around the age of six, this emotional brain is developing and predominant; therefore the relationships, connections and a child's emotional well-being are exceedingly important. Four-year-olds can tell you if he or she wants vanilla or chocolate ice cream. That choice is coming from memory and emotion. They like one more than the other. That's feeling and indicates the limbic brain is working well.

The cerebral cortex, the thinking brain, is the last to develop. Development begins about 6 or so. It takes 25 +/- years for the cerebral cortex to really develop fully and we'd consider them to be adult. The brain's growth is really a back-to-front process and, as you can tell, it takes time.

LESSON THIRTEEN

Facilitator decides whether to invite the three-year-olds to participate in this lesson.

SONG:
Facilitator and children sit on floor in a circle. Children and Facilitator sing "There's Just One Little Nose Like Mine". Facilitator endorses children as a class, such as "You've learned that song, children!" Facilitator says, "You are learning to find your own creativity inside you. That means you are having many ideas about how to do things. You are also finding that deep inside you there is lots of beauty and you are having fun."

SHOW:
Facilitator says "Name something in this room that is up high."

DISCUSS:
Facilitator chooses a child whose arm is raised. "Betty, point to something up high." Betty responds and Facilitator says, "Yes, the clock is up high." The Facilitator calls on two other children who desire to respond and repeats the same procedure. The Facilitator says, "Go find your own space children."

SHOW:
The Facilitator says, "Look at the clock. It is on a high level."

DISCUSS:
"What else in this room is on a high level?" asks the Facilitator. The Facilitator chooses a child whose arm is raised, and the child responds, "The top of the window frame (valance) is up high." The Facilitator says, "Yes, you are right." Two more children are selected to identify a different object on the high level.

APPLY:
The Facilitator says, "Go find your own space, children." Children respond. Then the Facilitator asks the children to do a freeze on the high level, using the objects the children identified as high. The Facilitator says, "Do a different freeze on the high level." The Facilitator says, "Do another different freeze as high as _____." Facilitator endorses children.

SHOW AND DISCUSS:
The Facilitator asks, "What is something in this room that is on the low level?" The Facilitator chooses a child whose arm is raised. The child points to a pillow. The Facilitator says, "Yes, the pillow is on the low level (or whatever the child identified). Two more children are selected to identify a different object on the low level. Then the Facilitator says, "Go find your own space, children."

APPLY:
Then the Facilitator asks the children to do a freeze on the low level, using the objects the children identified as low. "As low as _____." The Facilitator says, "Do a different freeze on the low level. A low as _____. Now, do one more different freeze as low as _____."
Note: Facilitator may need to remind some children to "Use all of yourself to get low."

Facilitator endorses children, "You did it, children."

JUMPING:
While clapping an accompaniment, the Facilitator says, "Find a way to jump, children." Facilitator describes what she/he sees. For example: "I see jumping with arms helping. I see jumping front and back. I see jumps turning." Do for about 20 seconds. Facilitator says, "Freeze, children."

STRETCH:
Children sit on floor with legs in front. The Facilitator says, "Press the backs of your knees against the floor, and touch your toes with your hands." Children respond. The Facilitator says, "While holding your toes and the back of your knees touching the floor, put your head on your knees." The Facilitator counts to three. Children sit up. The Facilitator says, "Wiggle your knees up and down to rest them." Children respond.
The Facilitator asks the children to do the stretch two more times.

ARMS: (Music, Sugar Plum Fairy from Nutcracker Suite by Tchaikovsky)
The Facilitator says, "Children, you are going to find your own way to move your arms. Find a space where no one else is and kneel on one knee." Facilitator puts on music and says, "Find a way to move your arms." As children respond, the Facilitator describes what she/he sees. For example: "I see arms go up high, then swing down to the floor." The Facilitator says, "Freeze," and stops music and endorses. For example: "I saw different arm patterns, children." The Facilitator says, "Move your arms down low. Now, move your arms up high." Facilitator endorses. Children sit on floor in a circle.

CONNECTEDNESS:
Facilitator asks children "What would happen if you had no arms?" If children don't respond, prompt with questions, "How would you eat?" Children respond. "How would you give a hug?" Children respond. "How would you play?" Children respond. Facilitator asks, "Children, are you happy you have arms?" Children respond. Facilitator says, "I am happy for my arms, are you?"

SIZE: (Music, Minuet in G by Beethoven)

SHOW:
Facilitator puts two crystals, one big and one little, on the floor in the circle where the children can see them.

DISCUSS:
Facilitator asks, "What colors do you see in these crystals?" Children verbally respond. Facilitator asks, "Children, do you like crystals?" Children verbally respond.

APPLY:
The Facilitator turns on the music and says, "Go find your own space and get big like this crystal is big". Facilitator holds up the big crystal and says, "Get this size, children." The Facilitator says, as she/he holds up the little crystal, "Get this size, children." Facilitator holds up little and big crystal three times. Facilitator endorses the group.

IMPROVISATION: (Music, Waltz in C-Sharp Minor by Chopin)
Facilitator says, "Dance any way you want to, until I hold up this little crystal. Keep your dance going while getting little. When I put this little crystal behind me, dance anyway you want to. When I hold up this big crystal, keep your dance going while dancing big. "Facilitator stops the music and says "Freeze." The Facilitator endorses the children. Children return to sit in a circle.

CONNECTEDNESS:
Facilitator says, "Children, how would you like to live in a world where everything was the same size?" Facilitator pauses so children can think. Facilitator continues, "What would happen if babies were the same size as their moms and dads? Would moms and dads be able to take care of their babies?" Children verbally respond. Facilitator asks "What would happen if bees were as big as moms and dads?" (Bees would kill us) Children verbally respond. Facilitator asks, "What would happen if kitty cats were as big as moms and dads? Would it be safe to have a kitty as a pet, if kitties were as big as moms and dads?" Children verbally respond. Facilitator asks, "Children, are you glad we live in a world where some things are little and some things are big?" Children verbally respond. Facilitator replies "I am too."

LEG LIFTS: (Music, Sugar Plum Fairy from Nutcracker Suite, by Tchaikovsky)
Facilitator says "Children, let's think about direction. Stand up please." Facilitator says, "Lift your leg backward." As children respond, Facilitator endorses "You did it children." Facilitator says, "Lift your leg forwards." As children respond, Facilitator says "Other leg forward." Each leg gets a turn two times. Facilitator endorses. Facilitator has all the children lift their legs the same way. Facilitator

says, "Children, lift your leg sideways." Facilitator changes and says, "Lift other leg sideways." The Facilitator has children do each leg two times. Facilitator endorses. Facilitator says, "Children, find your own space." Facilitator says, "You are going to do leg lifts to the front while doing a front arm freeze." Children respond. Facilitator puts on music and says, "Do leg lifts to the front," and repeats "Leg lifts to the front." When all have done it four times, the Facilitator stops the music and says, "Children do an arm freeze to the back." Children respond. Facilitator says, "While your arms are in a freeze to the back, do leg lifts to the back." Facilitator puts on music and says, "Do leg lifts to the back." When all have done it four times, the Facilitator stops the music and asks the children to do an arm freeze to the side. Children respond. Facilitator starts music and says, "Do leg lifts to the side." Children do leg lifts to the side four times. Facilitator may need to coach as both arms could go to each side or both arms to same side.

Facilitator endorses--for example, "You did leg lifts to the front, side and back with arm freezes." Facilitator asks children, "How did your leg lifts feel today?" Children respond (this is talking about feelings issue). Children sit on floor in a circle with Facilitator.

EMOTION FEELING: (no music)

SHOW:
Facilitator shows children a picture of a happy child.

DISCUSS:
Facilitator asks, "How does this child feel?" Children respond.

DISCUSS:
Facilitator asks each child, "What makes you happy?" Each child responds

APPLY #1:
Facilitator says, "Children, find your own space and do a happy freeze." Facilitator may need to coach if some child's face does not look happy. "Matt, how does your face look when you feel happy?"

APPLY #2:
Facilitator says, "Children, do a jump that tells me you feel happy. "Facilitator endorses. For example, the Facilitator could say, "All right!!" Children return to sit in a circle.

RHYTHM:
Facilitator says, "Today, we are going to talk about rhythm, another way to say rhythm is sound."

SHOW:
The Facilitator claps once while saying, "Josh." The Facilitator does this two more times.

DISCUSS:
The Facilitator asks, "How many sounds do you have in your name, Josh?" (one sound). The Facilitator claps and says each child's name in the circle who has one sound, such as Paul, Ann, etc. The Facilitator asks children to find their own space.

APPLY:
The Facilitator says, "While I clap and say the names, you do a freeze. Do a different freeze for each sound." The Facilitator then claps (slowly) and says all the names with one sound. (If necessary, the Facilitator can repeat the names until all the children have done one-sound freezes). The children return to sit in the circle.

SHOW:
The Facilitator claps two times.

DISCUSS:
The Facilitator asks, "Whose names match two sounds?" Facilitator claps and says, "Mil-lie, Ben-ji, An-drew." The children join in clapping and saying all the names in the circle with two sounds. The Facilitator goes slowly and pauses after each name, such as Mil-lie, pause. Ben-ji, pause. An-drew, pause. The Facilitator endorses, "Your freezes matched those names!!"

APPLY:
The Facilitator asks the children, "Find your own space." Children respond. The Facilitator says, "While I clap and say the names of children with two sounds in their names, you do a different freeze for each sound. Children respond. The Facilitator endorses.

SHOW:
Facilitator continues with clapping three sounds.

DISCUSS:
Facilitator asks, "Whose names match the three sounds?"

APPLY:
Children do three freezes to match these sounds while Facilitator claps and says, "Ann-ma-rie," "Glo-ri-a," "Al-the-a." Facilitator endorses, such as, "You've got it, children!"

Repeat/Show/Discuss, Apply for children who have four sounds in their names. Facilitator endorses.

IMPROVISATION: (Music, Minuet in G by Beethoven)
Facilitator says, "Children you may have a turn to dance to the music any way the music tells you to dance." Facilitator puts on music and describes what he/she sees (this is encouragement). When music stops, children freeze. Facilitator endorses.

Repeat Drug and Alcohol lesson from earlier lesson. Excuse any children who have not been cleared to do this lesson.
For subsequent lessons on Rhythm

SHOW:
Facilitator puts one piece of pink construction paper on the floor (the children are seated on the floor in a circle).

DISCUSS:
"How many sounds does pink have?" Facilitator asks children. Children respond verbally.

APPLY #1:
Facilitator and children clap and say, "Pink" several times.

APPLY #2:
Facilitator asks children to do a different freeze every time they hear Facilitator clap and say, "Pink." Children respond. Children return to sit in the circle.

SHOW:
Facilitator places a piece of purple construction paper on the floor.

DISCUSS:
Facilitator asks, "How many sounds does purple have?" Children verbally respond.

APPLY #1:
The Facilitator and children clap and say, "pur-ple" three times.

APPLY #2:
The Facilitator asks children to find a space. Children respond. As Facilitator touches the purple construction paper and says "pur-ple," the children find a different freeze for each sound. Do three times. Children return to sit in circle.

SHOW:
Facilitator puts down on the floor the pink construction paper to the right of purple construction paper.

DISCUSS:
The Facilitator asks children to clap and say the three sounds as Facilitator slowly touches each piece. Children find their own space.

APPLY:
The children will do a different freeze as Facilitator says and touches the construction paper: pur-ple (touches purple piece two times) and then pink one time. Here is the rhythm: pur-ple, pink, pause; then repeat and pause. Repeat four times. The Facilitator endorses.

LESSON FOURTEEN

By the end of this lesson the children will be able to do the following:

1. Sing songs without Facilitator's help.

2. Run with arms helping, while using the concept of direction

3. Stretch their legs in a new way.

4. Create rhythm patterns using names of children in the class

5. Learn the new concept of texture and how to apply it though movement.

6. Jump and stretch to relax the body.

7. Improvise while matching the music.

8. Answer feeling questions.

PURPOSES FOR LESSONS FOURTEEN

NOT for Three-year-olds: However facilitators may invite those three-year-olds he/she feels is ready.

1. The self-worth songs with their enriching support have a lasting, positive reflection on preschool children. What happens in the brain?

Brain Connections: As we have mentioned, the brain develops over time. The more we practice with the words in these songs and the more we hear them, the more impact on the brain. The rhythm helps reinforce and brings the brain into synchronistic harmony with itself.

2. Experiencing the exhilaration of running while adding another body part (arms) is exhilaration indeed!

Brain Connections: Movement excites a number of areas in the brain, many of which flow through the cerebellum for coordination. Adding more body parts, such as arms means more neurons are added, and more pathways for coordinating thinking.

3. Stretching relaxes the body.

Brain Connections: Stretching relaxes the body. Yawning relaxes the brain. It brings more oxygen into the system. Stretch, yawn and relax.

4. Because children have had success in learning previous concepts (because of using the concept process), learning two more concepts—rhythm and texture—will be an eager challenge. This lesson may, in reality, be an 18th or 19th lesson, as the Facilitator decides how often each lesson is repeated, before moving on to the next lesson.

Brain Connections: As we've mentioned, this curriculum combines a good deal of brain-related development. New concepts, new ways of thinking help children to feel comfortable in handling new situations. The more neuronal pathways, the easier it is to deal with the world.

5. To acquire the ability to learn through the tactile sense may fascinate the children as yet another way to learn.

Brain Connections: The sense receptors on the skin and fingers feel a tactile sensation and that sensation is sent to the brain for processing. Many parts of the brain are engaged in this new learning event. It tingles like when your foot's asleep.

6. While improvising, children will match the music by dancing fast when the music is fast, and slow when the music is slow.

Brain Connections: Improvising means letting go of any previous experience or memory and just responding to the music. The body and brain get in sync with the rhythm and both relax into the flow of life.

LESSON FOURTEEN

SONG:
Facilitator and children sing, "There's Just One Little Nose Like Mine." Facilitator says, "Children, you've learned that song!"

RUNS: (Music, Minute Waltz, by Chopin)
The Facilitator says, "You are going to do runs. If you would be willing to wait for your turn, please sit here," indicating his/her right side. "Those who do not want to wait, go find your own space, and do a freeze." The Facilitator says, "You are going to run forward in a circle." She/he puts on music and the Children respond. After six or seven seconds, the Facilitator stops the music and says "Freeze." The Facilitator asks, "Were you running forward?" Children verbally respond. (The Facilitator may need to coach a little because the children were running in a circle.) If any child seems confused, have the children run forward in a circle again. Facilitator endorses. For example, Facilitator says, "You are thinking about direction today, children!"

The Facilitator asks children to do a different arm freeze. Children respond. The Facilitator asks children to run backward in a circle. Facilitator puts on music and Children respond. Again, the Facilitator may need to coach a little. The Facilitator says, "Face the wall, children." Children respond. The Facilitator says, "Choose a different arm freeze, children." When children have responded, she/he puts on music and says, "Run backward to this other wall, children." Children respond, and freeze by opposite wall." She/he endorses, "You did it!" The Facilitator says, "The children who were willing to wait for their turn may now have a turn. The children who have had a turn may sit on the floor here," indicating with her/his arm, where these children are to sit.

Facilitator says to this group of children, "Choose an arm freeze." Children respond. Facilitator says, "Run backward in a circle." The Facilitator starts music. Children respond. Facilitator coaches if needed. Children repeat. Facilitator endorses. For example, "It is not easy to run backward in a circle, but you are working on it!" If all children did it, the Facilitator says, "It is not easy to run backward in a circle, but you did it!"

STRETCH:
Children sit on floor. Facilitator says, "Put your legs together in front of you. Lift your arms up high and reach over and touch your toes. Put your head on your knees (while touching your toes). "Facilitator counts to two to her/himself. The Facilitator says, "Sit up, children, and wiggle your legs." This will relax their legs. Do this stretch three times.

RHYTHM:

The Facilitator says, "We are going to work with rhythm today. Remember, another way to think of rhythm is sound. Whose names have one sound?" The Facilitator will clap and say child's name. For example: "Paul," as she/he claps once. Facilitator claps and says, "Ann." Children join in clapping and saying the names of children in the group whose names have one sound. If group is small with children whose names have one sound, repeat until all children do it.

Facilitator says, "Find your own space, children." Children respond. Facilitator says, "Find a freeze and do it as I clap a one-sound name." Facilitator claps and says, "Paul" (pause, as Facilitator says, "Do a different freeze each time"), "Ann" (pause), "Mark" (pause) "Ruth" and etc.
Facilitator says, "Sit down on the floor right where you are, children." Facilitator asks, "Whose name has two sounds?" Facilitator, without waiting for an answer, claps two times while saying, "Le-mah" (pause) "Ro-bert" (pause) "Beck-y." Children join in clapping and saying the names. Facilitator asks children to stand and do a freeze for each sound. Children respond. As the Facilitator claps and says "Le-mah" (pause) "Ro-bert" (pause) "Beck-y". Repeat until all the children can do it. Facilitator endorses, for example, "You are doing it!"

Facilitator asks children to sit in a circle on the floor. She/he says, "There are some children in our group whose names have not one, not two, but three sounds." Facilitator claps and says, "E-li-za," "Ben-ji-man," "Ann-ma-rie." Facilitator repeats until all children are doing it. Facilitator says, "Find your own space, children." Children respond. Facilitator says, "Do freezes as I clap and says, "E-li-za" (pause) "Ben-ja-min" " Ana-ma-rie." Since names with three sounds are more challenging, the Facilitator repeats each name twice. Facilitator endorses-- for example, "You are listening today, children."

If there are any children whose names have four sounds, repeat the procedure.
    a. After using names in subsequent lessons, use words, such as, "You", "me", "I like you", "we are friends," etc.
    b. Increase tempo slightly
    c. Add music

TEXTURE: (concept)

Facilitator and children sit in a circle on the floor. The Facilitator says, "Today we are going to talk about texture. Texture means how something feels when we touch it."

SHOW:
The Facilitator puts two shells on the floor and says, "These are shells. Shells live in the ocean. The waves move the shells on to the sand. The little fish crawl out and leave their shells."

DISCUSS:
The Facilitator says, "Tell me one thing about these shells." Children verbally respond. The Facilitator picks up one shell and her/his finger lightly rubs the smooth part of the shell, and says, "This part of the shell feels smooth when I touch it." Facilitator hands the shell to one child and says, "Feel how smooth this part of the shell feels." Child responds. The Facilitator takes the shell and hands it to the next child and says, "Feel how smooth this part of the shell feels." The shell is passed to each child in the circle.

APPLY #1:
The Facilitator says, "Children, go find a place to stand. Let your arms move as smooth as the shell feels." Children respond. The Facilitator repeats, "Let your arms move as smooth as the shell feels." As the Children respond, the Facilitator endorses, "Matt's arms are moving smoothly. I see Jared's are moving as smoothly as the shell feels. Rachel's arms are moving up and down smoothly."

If any child's arms get even slightly bumpy the Facilitator has those children go through the show/discus/apply process again until all the children can do smooth with their arms. Facilitator says, "Freeze." The Facilitator asks the children to "do smooth." While Children respond, the Facilitator says, "A smooth dance like the shell feels smooth.
The Facilitator continues endorsing as she/he describes how each child is responding while keeping the goal of "smooth as the shell feels" in the children's minds. The Facilitator says, "Freeze."

APPLY #2:
The Facilitator says, "Children, do a smooth dance using all of yourselves." Children respond. The Facilitator describes what she/he sees. Such as, "Matt is doing a smooth dance, etc." Facilitator says, "Freeze." Facilitator says, "Come sit on the floor."

SHOW:
Facilitator picks up the second shell and rubs a finger over the bumps and says, "This shell feels bumpy." The Facilitator hands the bumpy shell to a child.

DISCUSS:

The Facilitator says, "When you rub your finger over this shell, how does it feel?" Child verbally responds. Each child touches the bumpy parts of shell and says how it feels.

APPLY #1:

The Facilitator asks children, "Go find a space where no one else is and let your arms move as bumpy as the shell feels." Children respond. Facilitator repeats, "Move your arms as bumpy as the shell feels." The Facilitator endorses by describing what she/he says, such as, "Matt's arms are bumpy," until each child's response is described. Facilitator describes what she/he sees. Facilitator says, "Freeze."

The Facilitator says, "Come sit in a circle, children."

SHOW:

The Facilitator shows bumpy shell again and has each child touch it again.

DISCUSS:

The Facilitator says, "How does this shell feel?" Children verbally respond.

APPLY #1:

The Facilitator says, "Go find your own space and move your legs as bumpy as this shell feels." As Children respond., Facilitator repeats, "Move your legs as bumpy as this shell feels. The Facilitator describes what she/he sees, such as , "Matt is kicking his legs as bumpy as this shell feels." When Facilitator has described each child's move she/he says, "Freeze." The Facilitator says, "Now, children, let your arms and legs move as bumpy as the shell feels." Facilitator describes what she/he sees. Facilitator says, "Freeze."

APPLY #2:

The Facilitator asks children to do a bumpy dance (no music) like the shell feels bumpy. If there is even one child who does not do bumpy, have child(ren) sit besides you until the others "Freeze." The Facilitator takes the child(ren) through a different 'Show' step using a different bumpy shell. Then the Facilitator takes the child(ren) through 'Discuss' and 'Apply' steps. Facilitator endorses all the children. For example, "Children, you did it. You did it."
The Facilitator says, "Thank you, children. Go and sit on the floor."

JUMP: (big muscle)

The Facilitator says, "Children, while I clap, jump any way you want to." Facilitator chants, "Jump, jump, jumping children love to jump." Do three times.

STRETCH: (small muscle)

The Facilitator asks children to sit on the floor and put their legs together in front with the backs of their knees touching the floor. The children reach their hands up high and lean forward and touch their toes, putting their foreheads on their knees. While the children are in this position, the Facilitator counts to three. Children sit up. Then, children wiggle their legs to relax them. The Facilitator has the children repeat this three times.

IMPROVISATION: (Music, Nocturne in C-Sharp Minor by Chopin)
The third step in the creative process

The Facilitator puts on the music and says, "Children, you may dance any way the music tells you to." Children respond. Then, the Facilitator stops the music saying, "Freeze." Children hold their freezes until he/she says, "Thank you." Children return to sit in the circle. Facilitator endorses, such as, "Children, some of you were matching the music so well today! When the music slowed down, so did your dance. When the music got faster, so did your dance. When the music went up high, so did your dance. Tell me, children, how did you feel when you danced to the music just now?" Children verbally respond.

SHOW:
We are going to talk about high and low.

DISCUSS:
Facilitator says, "Tell me something up high." Children verbally respond. Facilitator then says, "Tell me something down low." Children verbally respond.

APPLY #1:
Facilitator asks children to do a freeze on the high level. Children respond. Then the Facilitator asks children to do a freeze on the low level. Children respond.

APPLY #2:
Facilitator asks children to dance again, saying, "When the music goes up high, you dance up high. When the music goes down low, you dance down low." Children respond. When improvisation needs to stop, the Facilitator says, "Freeze" and stops music. Children return to circle. The Facilitator endorses, "I saw you dancing any way you wanted to, but dancing up high when the music went up high, and dancing low when the music went down low. You are learning to match the music."

LEG LIFTS:
Do faster than before because it is the 14th lesson (or more). Refer to page 141 for Leg Lifts

EMOTIONAL FEELING:
Happy

SHOW:
Facilitator shows picture of a happy child.

DISCUSS:
Facilitator asks, "What is this child feeling?" Children verbally respond. Facilitator asks, "What makes you happy, Annmarie?"

APPLY:
Facilitator says, "Find your own space." Children respond. Facilitator says, Children, do a freeze that tells me you feel happy." Children respond.

SHOW:
Facilitator shows a picture of a child who feels mad.

DISCUSS:
Facilitator asks, "What is this child feeling, Benji?" Child verbally responds. Facilitator asks, "Benji, what makes you mad?"

APPLY #1:
Facilitator says, "Children, do a freeze that tells me you "are mad.'"

Facilitator may coach any child who needs it. For example, "Benji, do a mad face. Eliza, what do your hands look like when you feel mad?"

APPLY #2:
Facilitator says, "Children, do a walk that tells me you are mad." Children respond. Facilitator says, "Freeze—a mad freeze." If needed, the Facilitator can coach a child again.

Facilitator endorses group. For example, "Your faces looked mad; your arms looked mad- your walk looked mad."

IMPROVISATION: (Music, Opus 39 Waltz in A-Flat by Brahms)
Facilitator endorses, such as, "You are listening while dancing, children."

Children sing self-worth song, "I'm My Friend."

The Facilitator starts over with Lesson One.
Do only one lesson at a time.
Do lessons in sequence.

Glossary of Brain Terms

Brain Connections: Fear and the Amygdala

We've talked a great deal throughout this work about the brain and its functions. One of the most talked-about area is the amygdala. We have done so, because this area is often considered the source of many of our fears. What I have come to discover is that much of our fear is not based so much in the present, but what has been stored in memory, and is now being projected into a current situation. This operation requires more than just the amygdala reacting to the saber-toothed tiger jumping off the rock at you. It's more about what's been stored in the memory banks from the time we were infants. (Those memories can be good ones from childhood on, but only if the environment around us helps us to cooperate with others and provide us a number of experiences in which we can derive positive emotions, internal experiences and emotions that will eventually lead to positive projections when in the future we are faced with challenging situations.) It is my opinion that we, as the adults in a child's life, are responsible to provide as many of those positive experiences as possible. It doesn't take money or power to do so. It takes desire, commitment and creativity.

Coming from a family where alcoholism was an issue, it took me a great deal of time and a lot of energy to protect myself from any physical and/or emotional pain. Most children will figure out some way to do that. However, that "some way" may be hitting others, biting, tantrums, withdrawals or some other form of protection. As they get older, those strategies don't work well in the outside world. The protection strategies that once worked in childhood are now a significant problem and the reward of protection doesn't connect with the self-knowledge that they are safe. Their behaviors then begin to create their own problems. We, as adults, can provide experiences that don't require protective behaviors.

Brain Connections: Encouragement

Encouragement, described in this curriculum, allows children to feel their feelings and yet have another way to express them. The Facilitator/teacher is using encouragement in allowing those feelings to occur and directing an appropriate avenue to express them. The Facilitator/teacher doesn't say: "You're so cute" or "You're so clever." These are expectations that a child may become fearful they can't meet. This activates the overworked amygdala and creates more painful memories they just don't need. Saying "You did it. You didn't hit," simply recognizes what the child did, and calls forth something they can do again.

Brain Connections: Handling Tough Situations

On occasion, some children may have more specific issues. Some may act out more than others and you, as the teacher/Facilitator, may be at a loss. Here is a recommendation that may help. Breathe. Just stop and breathe. Slow down the activity, yours if possible, and breathe. Taking deep, slow breaths moves the energy from the limbic system to oxygenate the prefrontal cortex where executive function/decision making occurs. Taking action from the limbic system usually means fight or flight. You want to come from a place that gives you more tools and options. So give yourself some time and, quite literally, breathing room to choose a path that will work for you and the child. You are creating experiences that will remain with a child for a lifetime.

Brain Connections: The preschool years are about getting children ready to develop the ability to think. As Facilitators of this age group, it's up to us to provide the emotional environment a child needs for this time in his/her brain development. This is especially true if a child's non-preschool environment is particularly chaotic, whatever the reasons may be. Preschool is a place for a child to be safe.

We express deep gratitude to Edith Cameron, our music consultant, Virginia Tanner for her inspiration, Jenna Johnson for typing portions of the manuscript, Jennifer Victorino for the cover design, and Carrie Lyman for the two self-worth songs, and Rachel Shannon for the artwork.

For more songs contact www.britekids.com

CREATIVE AND CONNECTED
BIBLIOGRAPHY

Beattie, Melody, (1987) Co-Dependent No More, Harper Hazeldon.

Bradshaw, John, (1988) Healing the Shame That Binds You, Health Communications, Inc.

Brown, Victor L. Jr., (1989) Healing Troubled Relationships, Bookcraft.

Brown, Victor L. Jr., (1981) Human Intimacy, Parliament Publishers.

Chopra, Deepak and Tanzi, Rudolph, (2012) Super Brain, Harmony Books, Random House, Inc.

Covey, Stephen R., (1989) The Seven Habits of Highly Effective People, Simon and Schuster.

Dayee, Frances, (1984) Private Zone, The Chas. Franklin Press.

Dweck, Carol, Ph.D., (2007) Mindset, Ballantine Books.

Hari, Johann, (2015) Chasing the Scream, Bloomsbury Publishing.

Laura, Jana, M.D., (2017) The Toddler Brain, First Da Capo Press.

Newberg, Andrew, M.D. and Waldman, Mark Robert, (2012) Words Can Change Your Brain, Hudson Press.

Open Up the Well of Feelings, Music Educators Journal, September, 1971.

Samples, Joni, EdD., (2010) Parent Playbook Preschool, Engage Press.

Siegel, Daniel, M.D., (2012) The Whole-Brain Child, Bantam Books.

Studies Cited from Internet research:

    Dartmouth: Social Cognitive and Affective Neuroscience, Volume 10, Issue 3, 1 March 2015, Pages 364-370

    Hebb's Law, Donald O. Hebb

    Iowa: Iowa Now, Arrested development: How brain damage impairs moral Judgment

    This Is Your Brain on Music, Levitin

    Time Magazine: quoting the American Journal of Psychiatry

Wegscheider-Cruse, Sharon, (1989) Another Chance, Science and Behavior Books.

Whitfield, Charles L., (1987) Healing the Child Within, Health Communications, Inc.

Woodruff, Dr. Asahel D., Basic Concepts of Teaching, Chandler Publishing, 1962

Woodruff, Dr. Asahel D., First Steps in Building a New School Program, 1963 Working Paper

www.ingramcontent.com/pod-product-compliance
Lightning Source LLC
Chambersburg PA
CBHW080509110426
42742CB00017B/3045